Herbert L Aldrich

Arctic Alaska and Siberia

Or, eight months with the Arctic whalemen

Herbert L Aldrich

Arctic Alaska and Siberia
Or, eight months with the Arctic whalemen

ISBN/EAN: 9783337324360

Printed in Europe, USA, Canada, Australia, Japan

Cover: Foto ©Andreas Hilbeck / pixelio.de

More available books at **www.hansebooks.com**

ARCTIC

ALASKA AND SIBERIA,

OR,

EIGHT MONTHS WITH THE ARCTIC WHALEMEN,

BY

HERBERT L. ALDRICH,
WHO MADE THE CRUISE WITH THE FLEET OF 1887.

CHICAGO AND NEW YORK:
RAND, MCNALLY & COMPANY, PUBLISHERS.
1889.

COPYRIGHT, 1889, BY RAND, MCNALLY & CO.

ALASKA.

TO MY MOTHER.

PREFACE.

While living in New Bedford, I found a most interesting field of study in the whaling industry. Its records spread out before me a series of marvelous adventures and what seemed like foolhardy attempts to outdo human possibilities. The more I studied, the more fascinated I became. Finally I determined to put into print a few short sketches. This, however, was merely retelling what had already been told by other writers, for there are several readable books on whaling in general, and sperm-whaling, in particular. These books are, however, long since out of print, with perhaps one or two exceptions.

I found the subject of Arctic, or Bowhead, whaling untouched by any author except in a most general and meagre manner, although it offers richer material than other kinds of whaling. It is carried on in a region beset with inconceivable dangers and risks; and in a region practically unknown, for no writer has ever visited it, though whalemen had been there every year for forty years.

The moment seemed to me ripe to preserve this valuable material, for modern science is fast removing the picturesque excitement of whaling; therefore I have made the cruise and pictured the subject as comprehensively, yet briefly, as I could with my pen and camera.

I wish to acknowledge my indebtedness to the New Bedford and San Francisco whaling agents, for every courtesy that I could have asked for, and to the many whaling masters who received me with such cordiality and hospitality.

HERBERT L. ALDRICH.

SPRINGFIELD, MASS.

CONTENTS.

CHAPTER I.
Icing in Behring Sea.................................... 13

CHAPTER II.
Among the Siberian Eskimo......................... 42

CHAPTER III.
Along the Shores of Nakoorukland.................. 63

CHAPTER IV.
Whaling.. 90

CHAPTER V.
From Point Barrow, Home............................ 114

CHAPTER VI.
The Nakooruks.. 138

CHAPTER VII.
Some Typical Experiences............................ 188

ARCTIC ALASKA AND SIBERIA.

CHAPTER I.

ICING IN BEHRING SEA.

The *Young Phœnix* was one of the few ships belonging to the Arctic whaling fleet that did not sail in the fall of 1886, but was one of the first to sail in the spring of 1887. This was most fortunate for me, for it gave me an opportunity to see, at its best, the preparation necessary to fit a vessel for the Arctic cruise. In order to do this fitting thoroughly, each ship, in leaving San Francisco, cruises for a month or so in the Central Pacific.

I sailed from San Francisco on this ship on Thursday, March 3, 1887. The day was rainy, chilly, and squally, but we said our "good-bye," and before noon were under tow, bound through the Golden Gate. The beautiful harbor looked dreary enough. Heavy clouds overhung both shores. Frequent squalls stirred up a choppy sea and bedecked it with white-caps. A drizzling rain chilled us through and through. Huge waves tossed the good ship about and swashed over the rail upon the deck. The only sign of life was our little tug, puffing away as she would rise on the top of a wave, then disappear behind it. Adding to this the fact that we thirty-five men were bound to a region where three hundred lives had been lost in the past thirty years, and where millions of dollars worth of property have been wrecked, the occasion was far from joyful. Very few words were spoken beyond the necessary orders to the sailors. After we had passed through the Golden Gate, the little tug dropped us, tooted her "bon voyage," and disappeared behind a big wave. For the following twenty-four hours we struggled against a heavy sea, hardly getting out of sight of land. Then came a change in the weather, with favorable winds, and three weeks of as perfect weather as I ever experienced.

The *Young Phœnix* was a ship of 355.39 tons. Although young in name she was old in years, having been built at Rochester, Mass., in 1822; but in spite of her years she was a stanch, good vessel. Her crew was composed of thirty-four men, the captain, M. V. B. Millard, four mates, one boat-header, four boat-steerers, sixteen ordinary seamen, three green hands, a steward, cook, cooper, steerage boy, and cabin boy.

Our course lay in a southwesterly direction to the vicinity of the Sandwich Islands, then in a northwesterly and northerly sweep to the Aleutian Islands, or, as all whalemen call them, the Fox Islands.

Promptly on Monday morning, March 7th, work was begun in overhauling the whaleboats. Each of the five boats was, in turn, taken in hand, thoroughly scrubbed, painted outside and in, fitted with its sail, steering-gear and oars. The whaling apparatus was also looked over and put into proper shape for use. This work consumed three weeks. Then followed work on the ship's rigging. Every spot that showed, or threatened, weakness was made as good as new. Sails were patched, strengthened, or replaced by new ones; the hold of the ship restowed; in fact, everything made ship-shape.

It is astonishing what an amount of work

there is to do on a whaler, but it is far more astonishing how this work is done with the tools at hand. Fortunately nearly every forecastle contains a variety of artisans. In ours were a carpenter, a painter, and other men useful in the duties outside of a common sailor. But there were also men technically known as "stiffs," men whose capabilities are only developed in the direction of consuming an abnormal amount of "salt horse,"—as all salt meat is called—and ship-bread. One of the boat-steerers, who also shipped as engineer, proved a good blacksmith; and the boat-header, a man who had spent over thirty years in actual service on whale-ships, was general referee on almost any subject. If the cooper could not make an article that was wanted, the blacksmith or somebody else could. When a rope of a certain size was wanted, one of the mates rigged a rope-making machine out of an old barrel. And so it was, everything needed was made at short notice.

A whale-ship is no place for a passenger or any person who does not turn to and work. Yet time did not hang very heavily on my hands. There were a variety of most interest-

ON THE EDGE OF A PACK.—Page 21.
[The cakes in the foreground are about fifteen feet high.]

ing characters to study and an almost unlimited supply of subjects for my camera. Being provided with a Scovill detective camera, 700 films, and 250 Carbutt plates, I was prepared for all emergencies, and embraced many. The one character above all others that interested and amused me was the cooper. He was a Scotchman of rare rotundity and keen wit. One noontime as I sat on deck with my camera, watching for game, he appeared. The temptation was too strong to resist, and I photographed him. But ever after that when my "black ditty box," as he termed the camera, was aimed toward him, he would either run or conceal himself. The steward was another striking character, a good-natured, intensely superstitious, thick-skulled Portuguese. Every morning I waited in my bunk for his "Hey, senor! Rouster out!" At first his English seemed very bad, but after eight weeks of his hash for supper every night, I concluded that it was not in English that he needed to take lessons.

Was there ever a better place to study character than in the forecastle? Portuguese, Scandinavians, Germans, Spaniards, Englishmen, Irishmen, Americans; almost every nationality can be found there. The Americans we had were bright fellows, mostly ranchmen. Of course, there was the man who did the tattooing, the accordion-jammer, the yarn-spinner, and the rest of the famous sailor kind. Many of these fellows found a home in the forecastle such as they had not known for a long time, if ever; not only good shelter, but plenty of wholesome food, and, if needs be, warm clothing.

Many things proved sources of amusement besides the personnel of the crew. There were the birds that escorted us from San Francisco to the Aleutian Islands, "pilots" or "San Francisco pilots" as the sailors call them. These birds served to while away many an hour, especially when we threw overboard a string with a piece of salt meat tied to each end. One bird would gulp down one piece of the meat, but before he could reach the other piece, another bird would seize it and perhaps jerk the piece out of the first bird's mouth; and these two pieces of meat would go down and up one throat after another oftentimes for fifteen minutes before the string would break and two lucky birds get the meat, much to the envy of a dozen or more disappointed birds. These birds never desert the ship until the Islands are reached. There, however, they draw the line and seldom venture farther. When we returned in October they were apparently waiting for us at the Islands, and escorted us back to San Francisco. They are sleek-looking birds and very graceful when on the wing. Sailors feel that their journey will be a safe one when under the escort of these pilots.

The new men had to be taught the compass, and the rigging with its numberless halliards, downhauls, and braces. Two finback whales broke the monotony by boldly disporting themselves about the ship. They were too small, however, to bother about. Then the rats that infested the ship needed attention. Some sailors will refuse to go to sea in a ship that has no rats on board, believing that disaster is in store for her. But there was no cause for such complaint on our ship. Two weeks of reveling on the ship's stores was sufficient to condemn the whole rat tribe; and one calm day the deck pot was filled a third full of charcoal, every crack in the ship where it was possible for the fumes to escape, pasted over with paper

—molasses serving as paste—and the charcoal set on fire. The result was that flour bags were nibbled no more and the cat's occupation was gone.

From the time we reached the thirty-eighth parallel we experienced nothing but continuous gales of wind until we entered Behring Sea. For six days we lay off the Aleutian Islands waiting for an opportunity to pass through. We had one night of suspense with the barometer at 28.2, but nothing beyond a severe blow happened, and on the seventh day, the forty-third from San Francisco, we beat through Amoughta Pass, the "seventy-two" passage to whalemen, and entered Behring Sea. Clouds concealed the volcano and mountain tops on each side of the pass, leaving only the snow-clad shores of Amoughta and Seguam Islands visible. We could not even tell whether either volcano was in action. Being weather-bound here was not entirely without consolation, for we had four good meals from some cod-fish we caught.

One of the officers assured us that our situation was not a fraction as aggravating as beating off Martha's Vineyard twenty-one days, after a four years' spermwhaling cruise, with home—New Bedford—less than forty miles distant.

I left the Pacific Ocean, with its long, heavy swell, most gladly and willingly, for I had become an easy victim to its wiles. Three weeks of gales and rolling in the trough of the sea had not been conducive to a contented mind and settled stomach, but it added warmth to my greeting to Behring Sea, where there is very little swell except in a gale. Slowly and surely we worked our course toward Cape Navarin on the Asiatic shore, about latitude 62° 30′. Just a week from the day we entered the Sea we encountered the ice, and before nightfall we had done considerable "icing." From the crow's-nest it was discovered that we were on the edge of a pack, so, going southwest, we skirted it, and in the morning found ourselves among part of the fleet, five sails being in sight from the deck, all keeping off on account of a cold gale which had sprung up. The ice kept the swell down, but it was unsafe to attempt to make headway or enter any of the many "leads," any one of which might lead us into the pack, then close up and perhaps hold us prisoner for weeks, and carry us off to the southwest.

We had not seen a sail for fifty-two days, and it was a great delight to find ourselves among so many of the fleet, especially as several more sails could be seen from aloft. We could "speak" nobody, however, on account of the gale. It was simply "wear ship" all day long, so as not to be tangled up in the ice.

Everything seemed very strange; on every side was ice; at the northeast was the pack; at the west was the shore—high and snow-clad—just south of the bight under Cape Navarin. The thermometer recorded only twenty degrees above zero, yet I found it difficult to keep warm, when on deck, in spite of two winter suits of under-flannels, a heavy suit of clothes, a dog-skin vest, and a heavy overcoat. Leather boots were no protection at all, but native-made boots of hair seal proved a great comfort. The "icing" kept all hands busy. Two men were aloft in the crow's-nest to pick out a path for the ship, and watch for whales; a third was on the bowsprit, or try-works, to steer clear, as much as possible, of large cakes of ice, and the watch on deck was ready, at any instant, to wear or tack ship. As we wormed our way along there was a constant flow of commands: "starboard!" "steady!" "port!" "steady!" "let her luff a little!" "steady!" as we passed in and out among the cakes of ice. The days grew longer fast. It was light at three o'clock in the morning and dark at nine in the evening. When the weather was clear the sunsets were glorious. In the foreground would be an occasional ship to give life to the picture, while the ice and water would reflect every ray of color and intensify its beauty. A sunset at sea is tame in comparison, lacking the one essential feature, the ice.

"B-l-o-w," "b-l-o-w," came down from the crow's-nest late in the afternoon of the twenty-fifth. It was the first whale, and every man was electrified. The boats were made ready to "lower away," but the whale was in too much haste to wait to be caught, and disappeared in the ice. We on deck did not see the blow, but watched with anxious eyes some grampus's blowing instead.

Having letters for Captain Simmonds of the *Sea Breeze*, we ran up the American flag at the mizzen peak as a signal for him to "come aboard." He soon came along-side and invited us to "come aboard." Whalemen call this going aboard of each others ships "gamming." I had heard a great deal of talk about gamming, but this was my first experience of it. When we got aboard we found the captain's wife and four captains from other ships. The story of each master since leaving port was told, an occasional yarn was sandwiched in, and the "gam" capped by an excellent supper of fresh pork, egg omelet, fried oysters, beef tongue, lobster salad, fried and baked potatoes, hot biscuit, sugar cookies, cake, and preserved pear.

Two days afterward we pushed into the ice toward the land. One lead after another was passed through until noon, when we found ourselves facing a solid pack over a mile wide. The good ship poked its blunt stem into it, and after six hours of steady work, we emerged into a large lead on the other side. Several of the other ships were already there. The next day we lowered the boats five times and struck and killed one whale, but he was only a few feet from the pack, so we lost him.

It is a streak of good luck if a ship gets a whale south of Cape Navarin, and as the way was apparently open to get above the Cape into the Gulf or Sea of Anadir, we hastened on, and May 3d found us off the Cape. There we met the pack, so we ran back through considerable young ice into clear water again. In doing this we had a fair breeze, while at the same time another ship coming toward us from the south had a fair breeze. This shows how local the wind may be in these regions.

Late in the afternoon, bark *Jacob A. Howland* came up. She was boiling. When Captain Shockley, in answer to an invitation, came aboard to gam, he brought several pieces of whale meat. Cuts that come from along-side the backbone or the after part of the whale are very good eating. We had three chunks, and as they hung up under the boat-house they looked more like beef liver well smeared with blood, than any other kind of meat. The usual method of cooking this meat is in "whale-meat balls," although stews and steaks are also had. Steward put the meat through a sausage machine, spiced it with sage, savory, and pepper, mixed in a little chopped pork, then made it up into balls and fried it. The balls were surprisingly toothsome, and I did justice to them worthy an old whaleman. The flavor of the meat is peculiar and somewhat gamy, perhaps as near venison as anything else.

The bight where we were has the reputation of being a most excellent whaling-ground, but it is an exceptional year when the ships get there ahead of the whales. Now that we got the exceptional year we found that it was also exceptional with the whales, for not a spout or a breach could be seen. To remain where we were was to run the risk of being shut in, should an east wind come up and drive the ice inshore; but to return whence we had come was to run away from where the whales ought to be, and to run greater risks of being caught in a floe. These were the alternatives, for the pack was on one side of us and the land on the other. The presence of the many walruses and hair-seals, persuaded the captains of the half-dozen ships now there, to hold on for a few days, as these animals are regarded as forerunners of the whales. Between gamming and searching the edge of the pack for an opening to get through that we might push northward, time passed rapidly.

Most of the ships that go out "between seasons," that is, sail from San Francisco in November or December and spend the winter sperm-whaling, visit the Sandwich, Marianna, and other islands of the Pacific Ocean for supplies. These supplies include live animals as well as vegetables and fruit. Most of the ships get pigs and chickens. On board the *Sea Breeze* was a happy family of a bullock, a goat, a sow with a litter of pigs, and a few chickens. Gamming would not be possessed of the many charms it is, were it not for this fresh meat to vary the monotony of canned goods and salt meat. We made a start toward a collection of animals while here. We received a present of a pig from Captain Devoll, of the *Mars*, and a few days later several little pigs from her pig-ship. We also discovered a white fox cast away on a cake of ice, and catching him alive, adopted him into our family, hoping he would fill the vacancy caused by the death of our yellow dog. A third animal fell into our possession the same day. It was a seal, whose weight was estimated at but little under a thousand pounds. The ship sailed up to within a hundred feet of him, and then three well-aimed bullets did the rest.

The fierce, chilly, northwest gale that we encountered when first we met the ice, had died away. It was followed by some most delightful weather, more delightful, in fact, than that which we had experienced in the Central Pacific. That was weather in which one had to exert himself to accomplish anything; this was bracing and strengthening, making it a pleasure to undertake any work or exertion. The thermometer kept just above the freezing point during the day and a little below at night.

Whaling captains have a reputation for being most skilful navigators. Navigating in the ice is as much more of an art over navigating in clear water, as sailing a ship is over rowing a boat. To maneuver a ship from lead to lead, and among large cakes in an ice-floe, requires consummate skill, and it is a lesson that sailors of much ability and experience have to study long and hard to learn. Many and many a time it seemed to me that we must inevitably be stove, but just as many times my confidence in the skill of the captain has been found to be well placed. The ship would swing, or wear, about, often not more than touching the dangerous ice.

In a recent investigation by an insurance company into the loss of an Arctic whaler, the adjuster, an experienced seaman, called an old whaling-master up to testify, and asked him several questions. The master then put the following question to the adjuster: "Suppose you were on a lee shore in a gale where it was impossible to tack ship, where there was not room to wear ship, and you could not anchor, what would you do?" "Expect the ship to go ashore," said the adjuster. "I wouldn't," said the old whaleman, "I would take in the after sails, haul everything hard aback and box-haul her," (that is, back the ship out). The insurance was paid without further question.

The wind was doing its work in breaking up the ice-pack, and on the morning of the 7th, two of the ships were working past Cape Navarin in spite of the snow and fog, so we followed them. Before noon, the weather cleared up, then the wind died away. Toward night, however, the breeze sprang up again, and darkness found us about ten miles off Cape Thaddeus. There are two bays between these two capes, St. Gabriel and Ushakoff. In the former is a settlement of a few native families, not over half a dozen, if that. As the bay was full of ice, we did not stop. None of the natives were seen, but while passing Ushakoff Bay, we saw three native huts, and noticed that a big smoke was made, and a flag waved to attract our attention. Could we have looked ahead two days and seen what was to happen, we would have stopped to trade. Instead, however, we pushed forward, hoping to find a clear passage across the Gulf. The following night, we and four other ships were stuck fast in the ice. We were in the solid grasp of the pack that had swept in around us, and must wait patiently until it should open and let us out.

On the first day of our imprisonment, I determined to be neighborly; so taking one of the sailors for company, and for assistance in case of possible mishap, I started across the ice for the *Jacob A. Howland*. She was only a mile off, but there were so many cakes of rotten young ice, and so many holes of open water among the cakes of solid ice, that it took us two hours to get there. It was a wonder that we got there at all, for the ice was too treacherous, and the undertaking too risky. Many of the large cakes were from six to six-

ICING IN BEHRING SEA. 31

teen feet thick, while the young ice was only two to four inches thick, and too rotten to bear much, if any, weight.

It was much to our delight that the ice opened sufficiently on the fourth day to let us out. A strong northwest gale broke up the young ice and opened occasional leads, so that by night we were in open water. A forestaysail was all the canvas we had out until noon of the next day, the 12th. The wind had died nearly out, and with it the heavy swell that had been on since the gale sprang up. So sudden was the transformation that it seemed like going ashore in the midst of a storm. Eight sails were in sight, and all we could do was to drift about. Was it strange that several ships gravitated toward each other? There had already been gamming enough for each master to relate what had happened since leaving port. Now was the opportunity to tell what each wanted to do, and to retell former experience. Three days afterward I went on board the *Eliza* to spend a few weeks with Capt. Edmund Kelley.

There were ten of us ships gathered in a hole that extended nearly as far south as Cape

Navarin. At first it was large, but shifts in the ice made it smaller. The pack at the north disintegrated day by day, allowing us to work northward very slowly, but the ice filled in, about and behind us, and on the eighth day we were not out of sight of Cape Thaddeus. On the next day, however (May 19th), the ice opened so that several of the ships started ahead. Between a fierce northwest gale and the fields of ice, progress was slow, but perseverance carried us ahead into another hole, where we were prisoners, and but little better off than before.

At such times there was nothing to do but be patient and keep good-natured by gamming. There was not a whale to be caught, nor any possibility of getting anywhere to catch one until the ice opened. The captains would endeavor to console one another by telling of hearing a whale "sing." I at first took this for a sophomoric joke, slyly intended for me to bite at, so I kept quiet. But one day there was a rehearsing of experiences, and I found that the masters really believed that whales do sing. Captain Kelley was the first to discover this singing, but he was laughed at for it. In 1882,

"WE WERE STUCK FAST IN THE ICE."—Page 30.

several ships lay at anchor under Indian Point. As usual, the masters got together, and in the midst of their conversation, Captain Kelley broke in "There's a bowhead!" Everybody laughed about "Kelley's band," but he insisted that whales were near by, and he was going to give chase. One master suggested that it was the copper on the ship, another that it was seals, another that it was the ice, and so on. But when Captain Kelley took up anchor and set sail, every ship followed him. One whale was caught. Soon more singing was heard. The result was the capture of several whales. After having attention thus forcibly called to the singing, it was not long before the masters were on their guard for it. As singing is almost never heard in the Arctic, it is inferred that it is a sort of a call, or signal, for whales when making a passage through Behring Sea, to notify each other that they are bound north, and perhaps that the Straits are clear of ice. While Capt. Wm. H. Kelley was right-whaling in the Japan Sea in 1881, he put his ear to the line and heard the whale that he had struck give a deep, heavy, agonizing groan, like that of a person in pain. It has been known for a long time that humpback-whales, blackfish, devil-fish, and other species of whales sing, and that walruses and seals bark under water, and it is believed that all animals having lungs and living in the water, as these do, have their own peculiar cry, or as whalemen express it, "sing." Whenever a whale is struck by a harpoon, it is always noticed from the masthead that every whale in sight is "gallied," that is, frightened. At most times they disappear, but occasionally they simply jump, then settle back quietly to feeding, or whatever they may be doing. It is particularly true that sperm-whales take fright when one of their number is struck. No reason has ever been assigned for this sudden signal of danger except this "singing" theory. It is believed that when a whale is struck, its cry of pain is heard by every other whale within sight from aloft. In January, 1887, one of the *Eliza's* boats struck a sperm-whale, and instantly the whole school, which was three miles or more off, started for their wounded companion, and circling about it huddled together as if to ask "what's the matter?" With bowhead-whales the cry is something like the hoo-oo-oo of the hoot-owl, although longer drawn out, and more of a humming sound than a hoot. Beginning on F, the tone may rise to G, A, B, and sometimes to C, before slanting back to F again. With the humpbacked-whale, the tone is much finer, often sounding like the E string of a violin.

We reached the ice-pack before we had gone a third of the distance across the Gulf. Then followed another period of waiting. Between listening for whales, shooting at seals' heads, dodging ice-cakes, photographing, and having an occasional gam to "growl" from weariness, time passed, but it passed very slowly. I devoted myself assiduously to developing accumulated pictures, but even that could not lift the cloud of uneasiness that hung over us. We wanted to be up and doing, in spite of the fact that there was positively nothing to do but patiently wait. Steamer *Orca*, the most powerful ship in the fleet, came up and tried in vain to penetrate the pack, so turned back. With steam she could easily go back and forth in spite of weather, while we sailing vessels were dependent upon the winds.

On the evening of the 28th of May, a sail was sighted at the south, and in the morning there were six more. We recognized them as part of the fleet that had gone eastward in hopes of getting north along the Alaskan coast. They had found the solid ice-pack as far south as St. Paul's Island, so returned. With them came news from ships at the south, the two chief items being that twenty-one whales had been caught and that the *Stamboul* had been stove; not so seriously, however, but that she could be repaired.

This was the slowest getting anywhere I had ever experienced. On the first day of May we were one hundred miles below Cape Navarin. A week later we were off the Cape. Then we pressed forward and went perhaps fifty miles, but only to be beset in the pack and remain three days without moving a ship's length, except as the current carried us. Then a northwesterly gale carried us back below Cape Thaddeus. Four or five days later the ice opened sufficiently to allow of making an attempt to work northward, and in two weeks we had only gone about one hundred miles. During these two weeks we had sailed north and drifted south, sailed south and drifted north, in fact, gone in every direction. One current carried us to within sixty miles of the Anadir River, while another carried us off to the eastward. Finally the current settled down to a general northerly flow and carried us in the proper direction at the rate of from two to twelve miles a day. Local currents occasionally interfered. Thus the first day of June each ship lay tied up to a big cake of ice, and of the vessels nearest us, the *Hidalgo*, which was east-southeast in the morning, was carried to south by east by night. The *Abram Barker* was carried from north by east to northeast by north; and the *Northern Lights* from west half north to southwest by west.

To be bothered like this is an every-day experience to an Arctic whaleman, and it is a small part of what he must patiently submit to. A contrary current may hold him in the pack while ships about him make sail, and head for the whaling-grounds. Or while he is wearing and tacking about, waiting an opportunity to continue his course, he is harrassed by the feeling that probably other ships have got through the ice somewhere else and found whales. Possibly he may be within easy sailing of a passage through the ice—as it was afterward learned we seventeen ships were—but not know it. He is always in danger of having his ship stove, and must be prepared at any moment, day or night, to fight clear of ice, or flee from a threatened pack or approaching floe. These conditions come nearer the proper ones for spoiling a good temperament than any human being ought to be tempted with. Even the patient Job of old would have been sorely tried had he been an Arctic whaleman. To hang week after week on the verge of getting somewhere is far more trying to the patience than one could imagine who has not experienced it.

On the second day of June the weather was thick and some rain fell, but at intervals it cleared up sufficiently for land to be discerned. We still lay tied up to a big cake of ice, in spite of a longing to get nearer the shore, which proved to be Cape Aggen and vicinity, but the weather and pack were too thick. The *Hidalgo*, which lay a mile or so off, was found to have two planks in her bow stove above the water-line, and with this in our minds we forgot to worry about hastening on. Early the next forenoon, however, we set sail, in spite of the fog, and worked to the eastward in the teeth of a strong wind. We hoped, by running from supper-time to midnight, to reach heavy ice several miles ahead. Four of us ships were beating along, when we discovered the *Francis Palmer's* colors at half mast, ensign down; we had been dodging wicked-looking cakes of ice all day, and we knew in an instant that the ship was stove, so we and two others went to her assistance. A boat's crew and the ship-carpenter were sent aboard, and all assistance needed was promptly furnished. The captain and I went aboard a few minutes later and found that the damage was not serious, though there was a bad break in the cut-water, three feet below the water-line. Everything forward was moved aft, and the ship weighted down at the stern with casks of water, sufficiently to raise the stem out of water, so that the broken place could be reached and thoroughly repaired. After returning on board the *Eliza*, I hastily collected my traps and moved over on the *Hunter*, Captain Bernard Cogan.

The next morning I found a terrific north-easterly gale blowing, causing the pack to surround us. A strong current was carrying us swiftly along with the wind. For thirty-six hours we were thumped about from one cake to another. The wind whistled sharply through the rigging, and hail occasionally fell. Every element seemed to have conspired to make life miserable on deck. Another ship was driven helplessly down upon us, and for an instant it looked as though we would both be wrecked, but a cake of ice saved us. When the gale let go, we found ourselves in a vast field of ice fifty miles south. To set sail and get back again did not take long, but we experienced some good icing in doing it. Steam was got up in the donkey-engine, and by running lines to large cakes of ice in our path, then pulling ourselves along with the windlass, we soon emerged into the clear water beyond. Twenty-four hours afterward we were becalmed off Cape Behring.

An experience of Captain Cogan in 1886 is typical of what exertion a whaleman will make to prosecute and complete his voyage. In going through the Gulf of Anadir he broke a piece out of the *Hunter's* cut-water, but did not deem it necessary to stop and repair it. When off St. Lawrence Island, he was caught in a whirlpool, had the rudder-head nearly twisted off, and two of the pintles holding the rudder

A SANDY ROAD OF NATIVES.

broken. It was necessary to make this damage good; then he started on again. When off Icy Cape he struck bottom ice, knocking in six timbers six feet from the keel forward of the fore-chains. This caused a very serious leak, but by running all the pumps, and bailing, he got at the break and stopped two-thirds of the flow. Turning about, he went into Kotzebue Sound, behind Chamisso Island. The wind has a rake of ten or twelve miles there, yet it was the best retreat at hand. Nearly everything in the ship was landed on shore. The spars were then unshipped and made into a raft, which was firmly anchored at both ends with the two bow anchors, and then weighted down and steadied with casks of water. A strong southeasterly gale came up, making it necessary to undo all this work. But when all was again quiet, the raft was rebuilt, and with this as a wharf, the ship was hove down so that the keel could be reached, and the leak thoroughly repaired. Before things were stowed down again, another southeaster came on, but it was too late to do any damage. Up to the time of this mishap the *Hunter* had not caught a whale, but less than three months afterward she went into port with eleven whales.

CHAPTER II.

AMONG THE SIBERIAN ESKIMO.

Calms at sea often seem to come at the most inopportune times, but the one that held us off Cape Behring on June 8th, seemed opportune to me, for it brought aboard our first native visitors. Of late years ships have seldom gone as far west as this, but we did not wait long before two canoes, with a dozen or more natives in each, came along-side.

Whalemen have got to calling these natives Masinkers, from their word *ma-sink-er*, for good, and now they call themselves that. The Russian name for this section of Siberia is Tchouktchis; so, strictly speaking, I suppose these people are Tchouktches, or perhaps more properly, Tchouktchisians, but their distinctive name will probably always be Masinkers.

The first demand of nearly every individual native was for a chew of tobacco. Then each canoe must have a bucket of bread. Being thus comforted, the men were ready to trade the few furs of deer and hair-seal that they had. The men of importance went into the cabin to do their trading. One old deerman produced a piece of wood carefully wrapped up, on which were letters crudely carved. After some study we read the following on one side, "1887. J. B. V. Bk. Nap. Tobacco give;" and on the other side, "S. W. C. Nav. M 10 help come." We solved the mystery in this wise. When the bark *Napoleon* was wrecked in 1885, off Cape Navarin, only fourteen of the thirty-six men were rescued. Of the twenty-two men lost, some got ashore, but they were reported to be dead. Two were supposed to have survived, and perhaps more, but these two left a message saying that they were going southwest, hoping to reach Oliutorsky. Search was made last year for tidings of them, but without result. We interpreted the message as follows: That J. B. V. (whom we afterward found to be James B. Vincent, of Edgartown, Mass., a boat-steerer of the *Napoleon*) was still alive, in 1887, and that he wanted tobacco to be given to the bearer of the message; that he was still southwest of Cape Navarin, ten miles, and wanted help to come and rescue him. We gathered, from what the old man said, that several of the wrecked sailors reached the shore alive, but that all except Vincent had died. The language of Cape Behring varies so much from that of other settlements whalemen frequent, that conversation was very difficult. We decided that the only thing to do was to report what we had learned to the United States revenue cutter *Bear*.

I never saw better natured people than these natives. They laughed and joked continually, and such a motley-looking crowd; some dark, others very light. All were dressed in deerskin, some with one suit, the rest with two. In the former case the hair side of the suit was worn next to the body, giving the wearer a ludicrous appearance; in the other case the second suit is worn with the hair side out, making the wearer look a third larger, and more like an animal than a human being. All these second suits were for sale. The idea of buying a garment off a man's back seemed inhuman, but to these people trade was a matter of life or death, while the garment is easily replaced. All were bareheaded. The men and boys had the crowns of their heads shaved, or clipped, close like the Franciscan friars, and occasionally a head was shaved around the outside of the rim, or bang, of hair, making it of uniform width. Back of the ears there would often be a long lock or perhaps a bit of a pigtail braid. No beards were worn by the men; years of shaving with pincers in true Indian style having left their faces smooth, though an old man would now and then have a semblance of stubble, or some chicken-hearted fellow would find the growth of his mustache too much for his courage. The women wore their hair long and in braids. The men had their Russian pipes, at which they took frequent pulls, perhaps on account of the opportunity to beg matches and tobacco. A pinch of hair would be pulled out of the deer-skin clothing and stuffed into the bottom of the bowl, leaving only room enough for a large pinch of tobacco. Six or eight good puffs would be the limit to a pipeful. These the smoker would draw into his lungs without allowing a particle to escape, then belch forth with a grunt of satisfaction, reminding one of a locomotive just fired up, then giving forth its big puff and resultant "chew."

Each native wore a belt, fitting rather snug over a frock-like garment, which was loose, especially in front where it is pulled up through the belt, forming a sort of pocket or receptacle inside. If one were given bread or anything else, he would drop it down his neck into this receptacle, next to his body, or perhaps draw it through his loose-flowing sleeve. To get into this receptacle the arm is drawn through the sleeve, and whatever is wanted is either poked up through the neck or pushed out through the sleeve. A little pouch to hold tobacco is hung about the neck. Turquois-colored beads are scattered about in the clothing, in the hair and elsewhere, and strips of fringe and fancy needle-work are stuck on almost anywhere, especially inside the garment. Having been through the hands of the medicine men, these charms keep the evil spirits off and protect the wearer from harm. When selling a garment they are religiously cut off. If there happen to be none, then a strip of fur, or the ends of the strings are cut off, perhaps both. This is that the wearer may be able to replace the garment. Families sometimes have a peculiar way of, or place for, sewing these charms on;

or perhaps a peculiar pattern of needle-work. This smacks of heraldry.

All the natives were plenty familiar enough, and to them the captain was the man all-important. They would often trade with him for less than with anyone else. Anyone that wanted to speak to him would call "Cogan," "Cogan," until he responded, never mind what he was doing or how far apart they were. Late in the afternoon, an hour or so after these natives had gone, another batch from Cape Aggen came aboard to trade a little, but to beg more.

The next day we were visited by six canoe-loads of John Howland Bay natives. They took possession of as much of the deck as they wanted for themselves and their traps, then kindly allowed the crew to have what was left. We were scraping the gum off the butt ends of whalebone at the time, and the natives had a feast off the shavings. Many would stuff themselves full and carry loads of the delicacy to their canoes. I tasted the stuff, but only once. It was as I should imagine a decayed raw peanut would taste. As the day was very damp and foggy, the natives had their water-proofs on. These are made of strips of the intestines of seals or walruses sewed together. "John, the Fisherman," was the spokesman of the party, as he had been whaling and could murder English well. Many of the natives, he said, had not caught any seals for many weeks, and unless a good catch of some sort was made before winter they would starve to death. He was hopeful, however, and said: "By and by, one moon, codfish, catch him hook."

There is a general impression abroad that unprincipled traders sell liquor to the natives on both shores of Behring Sea, and that the natives so devote themselves to drinking this liquor that they allow the hunting season to go by, and thus bring starvation upon themselves. Undoubtedly there have been individual cases of this kind, but it is not a general truth. A little reasoning would show this. Many natives never touch liquor, yet they and their families starve with the rest. Before the appearance of the whalemen, the natives caught whales, seals, and walruses in great plenty at their very doors. Now hunters must go a long distance, and then are seldom successful. When the whaling fleet was two or three times the size of the present one, the increase of whales did not

A MASINKER AND HIS WIFE.—Page 47

keep pace with the number killed off, but now the majority of whalemen think that the annual catch is less than the annual increase. Nevertheless the whales grow more and more shy year by year, to the disadvantage of both natives and whalemen.

Cape Tchaplin, or Chaplin, is one of the largest settlements on the coast. It has thirty or thirty-five huts, and is where the whalemen do considerable trading. Their name for the place is Indian Point. It is a low, long sand-spit, with the settlement at the extremity. Back of it toward the foot-hills is the graveyard. Bodies are buried in shallow graves covered over with stones and earth, and in most cases deer antlers are used to mark the spot.

When we rounded the point a canoe came along-side, and "Shoo-Fly," one of the best English-speaking natives, came up on the house, and soon gave the captain all the news there was, and more, too. Seven whalers were already at anchor. The customary bucket of bread was given each canoe as it came along-side, and each occupant received his share to a fraction. It seemed as if every man, woman, and child in the settlement came aboard. Considerable trade was brought along in the shape of whalebone, ivory, and fox-skins, but particularly boots and skin shirts and coats. But for this trade it is very doubtful if these people could eke out an existence. During the winter they make a large number of Masinker boots of hair-seal skins, which are tanned or sometimes chewed to crimp or otherwise manipulate them. For this reason the teeth of the women (for of course they do this chewing, as most all of the hard work) are often worn down nearly to the gums. Coats are made of the young seal skins or deer-skins and shirts of fawn-skins. For trade, tobacco always comes first. Whisky would, but whalers seldom carry it. Then come arms, ammunition, flour, calico—the generic name for any kind of cloth—axes, knives, traps, files, needles, thimbles, combs, ship-bread, kettles, etc., etc. The natives make their own thread of deer sinew.

The Masinker of the Masinkers is Gohara, a man of not over forty years, tall and commanding, and by far the best specimen mentally and physically of his people. He is a great trader and prominent whaleman, having four boats. What property he is known to have would sell

for at least $50,000 in San Francisco. Not only
does he trade with the whalemen and others,
but he keeps a large supply of everything on
hand, and almost controls the general trade of
the natives, particularly that in whalebone.
He gets more credit as a trader, however, than
he deserves, the same as many other men in
this world get credit for abilities that belong to
their wives. He is a good trader, she is a consummate one, and no bargain is made without
first consulting her. Siwunka, for that is her
name, is a third wife, but she has complete
control of the household and takes her husband
entirely to herself, making the other two wives
slaves and workwomen, pure and simple. One
of her sharp tricks is to make each captain a
present of a fine specimen of needle-work, such
as a pair of gloves, or boots, a coat, or the like,
and in return she always expects, and receives,
twice or three times as much as she would receive had the transaction been a trade. I
wanted very much to have the couple pose, that
I might photograph them, but he declined, saying that I would take his picture and carry it
off to another land; then he would have to die
and go with it. I meekly accepted his reason-

ing, which left no room for argument, seated myself on the carpenter's bench, and soon had three fine pictures of him. As he did not understand the mystery connected with the "click" of my camera, and was unconscious of being photographed, I hope he will not be called upon to follow the pictures.

My camera was taken to be a medicine-chest, and such ailments as the majority of the natives were taken with were never thought of before. They would come to me groaning, and say "Doghter," "Doghter." When I told them I was not a doctor, they intimated that they knew better. I fairly had to steal what pictures I got, for old and young were suspicious of the black box, particularly women with babies. To get a child in a fair light was practically impossible. The women generally perched on top of a cask under the house, or squatted down Turkish fashion in some dark corner.

What was ludicrous about these people was the manner and ease with which they would go to sleep. I saw a boy walk up to a barrel that stood on end, pull his frock up over his head, then drop face down on the end, and in a minute or two he was snoring away as contentedly —in spite of the fact that he was standing up— as though he were snugly tucked away in a feather bed. Some sleepers would draw their heads entirely into their deer-skin frocks; others would drop anywhere as they were.

The babies did not neglect the opportunity to exercise their lungs occasionally. Almost as soon as a child is born, it is sewed into a skin garment, with legs and sleeves, though the ends are sewed up so that the hands and feet shall not be exposed. A trap-door arrangement brings up the rear of the garment. When old enough to walk, the youthful Masinker has use of his hands and feet, and he struts about in a big pair of boots, taking up almost as much room as his mother. When he is heated from exercise and carrying his heavy furs, the neck-string is loosened, and the garment thrown back, leaving his shoulders and one arm bare. How it is possible for a child to live with this alternating of overclothing and exposure, I can not conceive.

Most of the women and girls wear strings of beads in their ears, not in the lobe as earrings are usually worn, but from half an inch to an inch higher.

The garments of the women and girls are loose trousers, and sometimes a waist of deer-skin, then a frock of deer-skin, and over this frequently a calico gown. The neck to the frock is cut loose for convenience in nursing.

In the afternoon I went ashore. We found plenty of scraggy-looking curs around every hut. Some barked at us, but the majority were too sleepy to be troubled about anything. The huts are made for the most part of walrus hides stretched over a wooden frame-work, averaging about eighteen feet in diameter, and being ten feet or thereabouts high.

The door and doorway are of wood, and boards from wreckage in many instances form most of the sides of the huts up to a height of five or six feet. Gohara's hut was covered with canvas instead of walrus hide. It has become a question here what to build huts of, and many natives think they will soon be forced to dig holes in the ground to live in, walruses have become so scarce. It is now necessary to go to St. Lawrence Island, fifty miles off, to get walruses. Owing to the scarcity of hides, a native woman, with a common knife, will split a hide as skilfully as ever leather was split. I went into one hut, not a very poor nor very good one. The sides were part board and part walrus-hide. Overhead there must have been an average of two or three holes to the square foot. I doubt very much if all the snow could be kept out in winter. Opposite the entrance, and occupying a quarter of the space inside the hut, was an inner apartment formed by deerskin hangings. It is a complete hut in itself. It is here that the occupants all sleep, and if it smells half as bad again as does the outer room, it must be very warm, for I doubt if Boreas could induce his forces to associate with such company. Nearly every hut has a framework lean-to back of it, on which walrus hides are stretched, and canoes, sleds, etc., are stored.

Many canoes are also strung upon lines between double rows of whale's jawbones, which stand twelve to fifteen feet high when firmly planted in the ground. We also found many ruins of winter habitations underground in which the large bones of the whale were used for the frame-work. Some of these ruins are used as caches in which to keep the winter's supply of food.

In front of every hut were children and old women, who begged tobacco. When I gave them to understand that I did not use the weed, they gave me to understand that I was wandering very far from the truth. As every Masinker uses it, even the suckling babe chewing a piece between meals, one who does not use it is beyond their comprehension.

As the whalemen visit Indian Point every year, and occasionally ship a few men as sailors for the season, there have come to be several expert whalemen in the settlement. As a consequence, the improved methods of the ships have been adopted quite generally, there being nearly a dozen regular whale-boats bought from the ships, in service, in addition to all their canoes. The method of the natives in whaling is ingenious. Whole seal-skins are filled with air, making large air-bags called "pokes." These are fastened on seal-skin lines six or eight feet long, one or two being attached to each harpoon. Each canoe carries four or five of these pokes, and another with a line one hundred feet or more long, which shows the

GOHARA AND ANOTHER MASINKER.—Page 50.

course of the whale should it attempt to escape. Three canoes usually go whaling in company, and as many of these pokes as possible are fastened into the whale, fifteen being sufficient to float it. An ivory or steel pointed lance is used to kill the whale. An important feature of this system is the yelling. It may not kill the whale outright, but it frequently gallies it so that it becomes an easy victim. A line is run ashore from the whale when it is killed, and everybody helps to haul the carcass up on the beach. Then follows a veritable picnic, a time devoted to shouting and eating. Every person who took part in the whaling gets a share or "lay." There is an old story among whalemen that the St. Lawrence Island natives pounded whale-blubber to extract all the oil and fat, and left nothing but the fiber and sinew, which made a good substitute for skins, and was used for clothing. While some of the Indian Point natives follow the methods of the whalemen, a modification of both methods is mostly used. In other settlements the poke method is the only one used.

Captain Cogan shipped three men here for the season; "Shoo-fly," or, as he called himself on state occasions, Mr. Shoo-fly (who, by the way, must have been named by some one who knew him well, as I got to, or who accidentally had a keen thought), "Jim," and "Lew." They were very proud of these sailor-given names.

A native not only wants to see everything, but he wants to do what the white men do, and have what the white men have. One ambitious fellow wanted a captain to bring him an upholstered sofa for trade. Many times I was asked to "see" what was inside my camera. One of the first requisites made of me was the loan of my handkerchief to a man sorely in need of one for immediate use. All the boys and girls were constitutionally hungry, and asking everybody for something to eat.

The odor about everything Masinker is far from pleasant and agreeable. If two or three of them remain in the cabin very long, the average white man wants to get out. One cause for this is a lack of the virtue of personal cleanliness, principally because they have no soap, and a most disgusting substitute. One of the happiest boys we had on board was one who had his hands washed with soap and water.

Of the excrements from the body, the Masinkers save one, not only to tan skins with, but to wash dishes, scrub house, and even wash their faces and hands. If cleanliness results, it is not satisfactory to the average nose, whether or not it may be to the eyes.

Leather is well tanned in this way by soaking for twenty-four hours or so. A long and thorough airing is necessary in order to make skin clothing bearable for most white men to wear, and the offensive smell is never entirely removed. The wonder is that these natives are not more disgusting and offensive than they are.

I learned of an interesting superstition while at Indian Point in regard to the species of whale called "killers." These animals are only about twenty feet long, yet they will kill a large whale, and as the natives sometimes find a carcass thus killed, they most naturally venerate the killer. To destroy one is to cause the death of many people as a punishment. I was told of an instance when a great many St. Lawrence Island natives died because one of their number caused the death of a killer. The natives believe that the killers live in the mountains in the winter, and that the various warm springs there are made for them to do their cooking in. Whether the killers are supposed to go overland, or through subterranean passages, or only in spirit to the springs, I could not learn. The St. Lawrence Bay natives believe that the killers have a house back in the mountains where they live winters. To keep in favor with the killers, the natives make knives of whalebone or ivory, and throw them into the water to aid the killers in killing the whales. In telling of this, my informant said: "We throw him knife, he wag him tail, and look blue," indicating that the killer is very glad to be thus noticed. In times of want, the medicine men go through a prolonged ceremony calling upon the killers to kill a whale near by, and thus relieve the distress.

We spent a day or two here, then hurried on to St. Lawrence Bay. These natives have less opportunities than do the Indian Point natives to catch whales, and it is probably on this account that the women have become so skilful at needle-work. Our stay here was only a few hours, and we hurried along, and on the night of the 14th ran into the bight under East

Cape, and anchored. Six of the steam whalers were already there. Of course, several canoe-loads of natives came aboard for bread and to beg, or trade. They had considerable walrus ivory and some deer-skin clothing.

While ashore here I was impressed with the strangeness of my situation. I was in bleak, dreary, forbidding Siberia, at the very extreme of the vast domain of the Czar, wallowing about in the snow and among a strange people who hardly seemed human. Between me and home was one of the best ships in the fleet, yet as frail as an egg-shell in the clutches of an ice-floe, which might appear at any moment. I wondered if, perhaps, there might not be Nihilists skulking round, or a Russian officer on the lookout for one behind some hillock. Perhaps a sudden blow might compel the ship to seek safety in flight. How would my companion and I fare then? Off to the northeast was a straggling bit of the greatest empire on earth, the "Big Diomede." Beyond was the "Little Diomede," hardly more than a gunshot from the other, yet under the shadow of the stars and stripes; while in the distance, distinctly to be seen, was Alaska, another barren region, but of a more hospitable blueness than the Asiatic shore had ever been.

We lay here four or five days, hoping for whaling, but were disappointed. Two or three whales were caught, but in a contest with eight or ten more ships, and most of them steamers, prospects for success were slight. While hesitating what should be the next move, a strong gale forced us to put out to sea. We beat about in this gale for two days, then, as the weather cleared up, made a few hours' visit off the Big Diomede, Ratmanoff Island, as the chart calls it.

June 23d we were thirty miles below Port Clarence on the Alaskan shore.

CHAPTER III.

THE SHORES OF NAKOORUKLAND.

The beach off which we lay was strewn with driftwood, and, as fuel was getting low, we dropped anchor, and took aboard several boat-loads. Then we made sail and were soon in Port Clarence, the mid-summer rendezvous, where we found half a dozen vessels already at anchor. Natives were aboard by the time the anchor was down. One glance showed that they were a great improvement over the Siberian natives. They were more intelligent appearing, dressed in better taste, not such pestiferous beggars, and cleaner. I asked to photograph Kooblu and his family. He is well known among whalemen as an interpreter, and his wife is excellent at sewing. But they refused, on the ground that they wanted to go ashore and take a bath first. The woman said she had been doing house-work, and her hands were all "smoke." The next day they came off dressed in their best, and as clean as soap and water could make them. One fellow asked for a match to light his pipe, and accepted it with a very polite "thank you." In fact, a minority neglected this little courtesy. Cloth is very generally used here for clothing, some natives having enough for only one garment, others enough for a full suit. It is in demand, as well as towels and soap. One woman had a regular dress and a pair of corsets. She could not understand the use for the latter, and even after being shown how to wear them, she threw them aside, exclaiming "*peechuk*," "no good." But of the former she was very proud, though hardly graceful in her way of wearing it. When sitting down she would take pains to save her skirt at the expense of her deer-skin trousers. When sewing, the skirt would be rolled up about her hips, out of the way. All Eskimo women, when sewing, as far as I observed, hold their work between their knees, or by one foot resting on it just above the knee of the other leg.

These Nakooruks differ from the Masinkers not only in appearance, but in customs and language. In winter they live in an underground hut called an "igaloo," and in summer in

A TYPICAL MASINEER HUT.—Page 51

a tent made of common cotton cloth, or, in exceptional cases, of skins, called a "toopick." There is no regulation form of these, but the most are oval, like the crown of a hat or an Indian "wickiup." The frame-work is of willow twigs, bent over and stuck in the ground, all joints or places where they overlie being lashed with strips of seal-skin. When regular tent-shape, there is the usual frame-work. We found many settlements about these shores, partially because of the presence of the ships, but more particularly on account of the fishing. Herring, tomcod, salmon trout, and "leather jackets," are very plenty, and soon after the ships depart the salmon run sets in. The seines used are made of strips of seal-skin with meshes of an inch or so. The knotting is as regular as though done by machinery.

Just off where we anchored was a settlement of about twenty toopicks, and I went from end to end of it without being once asked for tobacco or anything else. The dogs did a fair share of howling, but the children behaved well and were respectful. They were not as dirty and disgusting as the Masinker children. Many of the men wore an outside shirt, a sort of jumper, that was once white, and either seal-skin, or cloth, trousers, rather tight-fitting. A few of them shaved their heads on the crown, but this is not a general practice. Those that did not have a cloth shirt, wore one made of squirrel-skin. The garment of the women is of deer-skin, and it extends nearly to the knees. It is cut up at the sides nearly to the hips. Their trousers are of deer-skin, but tight fitting, instead of the baggy Masinker trousers, and with boots, or covering for the feet, a part of the garment. Instead of suspending their trousers, all Eskimo fasten them about their hips with a seal-skin cord; not, however, just above the hip-joint, as one would suppose, but two or three inches below. This results in a deep crease or groove in the flesh.

Most of the men are beardless, but mustaches are not infrequent, and a considerable apology for a full beard is occasionally met with. The tobacco habit here is as inveterate as on the Siberian shore, but the pipes are less elaborate, though of the same pattern. Perhaps the one thing that gives these natives an improved appearance over the Masinkers is the custom of carrying a bag over the shoulder as a catch-all, instead of bulging out the blouse over the pit of the stomach. The turquois bead holds its position in the veneration of these people, but not much external show is made of it. Although such a comparatively short distance from the run of whales, no attempt is made to catch any. In fact, they do not know how to. This limits trade here to fish and furs. The food is almost entirely of fish and seal meat, with occasionally walrus meat, and the whale meat brought by the ships. Nearly every man has a "kyack" to go about in. This is a most useful conveyance, but a treacherous one. It is made by stretching seal-skin over a wooden frame-work, something after the pattern of our canoes. It is barely large enough to hold one man. A single paddle is used. With dexterous handling great speed can be obtained. Kyacks are not used at all on the Siberian shore, but are in great use all along the Alaskan coast.

Babies here have a harder lot than any babies ought to have, though no more so, perhaps, than among all Eskimo. I saw some that wore only the clothes they were born in; others had a little shirt reaching nearly to the hips, and now and then one would be the fortunate possessor of a hood, and possibly a pair of boots. The children would usually be tucked away in the mother's garment, with their little heads either peeping up over her shoulder, and their large black, sparkling eyes wide open with wonderment, or they would curl up with only a bit of their faces visible, and sleep contentedly. They are held in position by a belt around the mother's body which lies across her breasts, and is tied just above the small of the back. To nurse the child, it is drawn out of its retreat and pushed up inside the garment from below; or, if the weather is chilly, the belt may be removed and the child moved about to the proper position under the clothing without exposing it to the air. Owing to the peculiar methods of nursing, on both the west and east shores, the breasts of the women are abnormally long.

Most of the women tattoo themselves. On the Siberian shore the women often have lines tattooed across the forehead, nose, and chin; also two or three on the cheeks, besides bracelets and fancy patterns the whole length of the arms. On this shore the women limit the tattooing to one broad line, or possibly two narrow ones (but more commonly to a combination of these, the broad one in the centre), from the lower lip down the face of the chin. Many girls are not tattooed now, the parents desiring to have them " alle same San F'lisco," as Kooblu told me. Several men have been taken down to San Francisco by the ships and brought back the next season, thus practically demonstrating the good intentions of the white men in coming among them. This has smoothed off many rough points in the untamed Eskimo nature, and resulted in their coming gradually to have more regard for personal cleanliness and comfort. A few of them make daily use of soap and water, and many of them take a wash whenever opportunity offers.

The barbarous custom among the men of wearing labrets or ornaments in the lip is slowly dying out. I did not notice any victims of this mania on the west shore, but a majority of the men on this shore wear a stone or glass button-like ornament just below one corner of the mouth, if not at both corners. Some men have thrown aside this disfigurement, which is exceedingly hideous. Only a minority of the young men indulge in it. Some have once worn them but discarded them, leaving bad scars where the holes have been allowed to grow over, while others never had their lips pierced. The farther north we went the more prevalent the custom was. One old man wore a piece of ivory four inches long at one corner of his mouth, giving him the appearance of having a tusk in his lower jaw like that of a wild boar. A pastime among the wearers of these ornaments is to take them out and replace them, and occasionally run their tongues out through the hole.

Nearly everything portable is carried in seal-skin bags, made of whole skins. The noses are tied up, and when laced properly at the opening, which is a slit between the two flippers, they are practically water-tight. These bags are slung over the shoulder by a string.

Captain Cogan made an excursion inland while we lay here, taking with him the three Masinkers from Indian Point, and three more frightened men than they, never lived, before the journey was ended. It seemed to them that the trip was for the one purpose of tormenting and killing them, yet they begged permission to go.

There were no suspicions of the white men, but every Nakooruk was watched with a keen eye. From one or two stray remarks, afterward dropped, we surmised that there may have been a contest at some remote time between Nakooruks and Masinkers, in which the former came off victorious. But, however this may be, these three men thought they certainly were doomed. They would have returned alone but for a great terror, the Nakooruk devil. One of the party was taken sick, and this means to an Eskimo the presence of evil spirits. Lew said he was afraid to return alone because "me meet Nakooruk devil, me no save him, he no save me." That is, the devil would talk a strange language, so he could not understand the reasons Lew would give for being away from his own people and among these. Afterward, in telling about his devil, Lew said: "No devil, Indian man no die." It was impossible to learn more about this devil. Masinkers are more superstitious than Nakooruks, and some of them live in great terror, fearing the devil or some other unseen enemy. Many of them sleep with their rifle at hand for ready use. When Captain Cogan went ashore at East Cape, he suddenly awakened a sleeping native. The fellow jumped, cocked his rifle, and covered the captain with it. But before he shot he came to his senses, comprehended the situation, and dropped his weapon. The year the captain lived among the Masinkers he found this terror of some unseen enemy very prevalent.

The Arctic seems to be a healthy place for mosquitoes, for not only did we find them in great force, but of unnecessarily large size and of consummate fighting ability. Their bite is poisonous to animals as well as to man. The natives have to protect themselves from them while living in the low lands, and they dig holes in the ground for their dogs to retreat to. Deer are sometimes driven to the extremities of sand spits to escape these pests, and the natives take advantage of such situations to secure a large supply of venison. Bears are claimed to become so worried by them as to wade into the water in a morass, or swamp, and be drowned in their efforts to seek relief. I was on shore frequently, and my experiences were such that these statements do not seem overdrawn to me.

Wherever I went ashore the flowers seemed

TOWING ASHORE THE EMPTY CASKS.—Page 74.

to be different from what I found elsewhere, and in such abundance and variety as I had never seen, not even in New England or Central New York. The colors were principally white, but there were both blue and yellow in many shades, besides other colors and combinations of color. The clear, deep, sky blue blossom of one species of moss was more exquisite than arbutus. Most of the flowers were odorless, but four or five kinds were noticeably sweet-scented. On the shores around us I found twenty-five different varieties of blossoms, most of them new to me, though there were the hypatica, forget-me-not, anemone and phlox. Such a garden spot in these Arctic regions seemed an inconsistency.

Nearly every canoe that came along-side had either fish or furs to trade, those from the vicinity having the former, and those from Cape Prince of Wales, King's Island, Norton Sound, and other distant places, the furs. It is understood at all these places that the ships are at Port Clarence about the first of July, so hither the natives come with their trade. In some of the nearer settlements all household goods are packed up, and the whole family moves here to be near the fishing grounds. A smart man will have an igaloo at two or three different places, and go from one to the other whenever there is a run of fish. In the same manner he moves about in the summer with his toopick. Fish are preserved either by drying in the sun, or by burying in the sand, to keep them at the freezing point.

Near the east end of the Port is a small stream, where the ships get water, and thither we went when our turn came. A dozen or fifteen casks, with a capacity of one hundred or more barrels, would be towed ashore, filled with fresh water and towed back. It is a good day's work to get off three rafts of casks. We got six hundred barrels of water.

When the *Hunter* sailed, I moved to steam whaler *Balœna*, Capt. George F. Winslow. The revenue cutter *Bear* was expected every day, and I was anxious to report the story of the unfortunate castaway at Cape Navarin. I was also anxious for letters from home. Our first mail since leaving home was expected by both the *Bear* and the tender to the whaling fleet, and was overdue many days. This made waiting tedious, though the weather was delightfully pleasant, the thermometer ranging from fifty to eighty degrees above zero in the sun. A number of the sailors went in bathing by jumping overboard, apparently enjoying themselves very much, though it was noticeable that they did not remain in the water very long. The effects of the hot sun told on the southern slopes to the hills, where vegetation struggled hard to throw aside its sere garb for a more verdant one. The hills had the appearance of the hillsides of New England in early spring, when the grass starts.

Natives came aboard nearly every day, and a few fox, otter, beaver, or lynx skins were occasionally bought, also fancy carved ivory pipes, made by the young men, and little bags decorated with fancy needle-work, made of various kinds of skins by the girls and women. Some of the carving showed a decided appreciation of form, but most of it was crude. Each native is said to keep a diary of his hunting trips by carving the important events on a piece of ivory, showing his camps, shooting deer, walruses, seals or bears, or catching and drying fish. A few of the supposed diaries were offered for sale.

One event happened ashore which shows the Indian nature in some of these natives. Saxy, a Sledge Island native, is one of the most prominent traders along the coast. He had a grudge against a Cape Prince of Wales native for stealing one of his wives. Happening to meet the fellow here, Saxy promptly shot him. Fearing violence from the man's friends, Saxy gathered his followers about him and started for home. Luckily the other party started homeward for fear of more shooting. Should this man's friends ever see Saxy, they will attempt to kill him, for a life must answer for a life here.

Whalemen never neglect to observe the Fourth of July, but our celebration could not begin at sunrise in this land of the midnight sun. The colors were set early by all the ships, and Capt. S. P. Smith of the *Wanderer*, gave a dinner to all the masters and their guest. Three days later the bark *Pearl*, our tender, hove in sight. Mail was what everybody asked for first, then followed inquiries as to what was going on in the world. Promptly the next morning we took our first turn along-side the tender, got our quota of coal and other supplies, shipped the whalebone, then retreated, and anchored in order to have time to answer our letters. The catch of the fleet, as far as reported, had been fifty-three and one-half whales, the half being the share of a ship which had divided with the natives. This tender was to take down about one-half of the catch of whalebone and oil, which, with the trade, would make her cargo represent a quarter of a million of dollars.

On the morning of the 9th the United States revenue cutter, *Bear*, Capt. M. A. Healy, emerged from a dense fog and dropped anchor a short distance from us. As soon as discovered, she was saluted by a blowing of whistles and running up the American flag. Captain Winslow and I immediately went aboard and reported with much satisfaction, "No disaster so far." I related to Captain Healy the story of the poor fellow at Cape Navarin, and he gave orders to prepare to sail the next morning to search for him.

No cutter in the revenue service can have a more hazardous service to perform than does the *Bear*. Formerly many trading vessels infested the whole Alaskan coast. They were run by a set of miserable scamps who sold the vilest of whisky to the natives, and robbed them of their hard-earned furs, whalebone, and other trade. These men are now weeded out. Though these men made large sums of money, I am told that hardly a one of them has lived to enjoy his ill-gotten gains, either being shot, or drowned, or losing the money through drink or other cause. Since the appearance of the cutter these scamps have disappeared. What trade there is now the whalemen get legitimately. Our Government makes a grave mistake in prohibiting the selling of good rifles and fixed ammunition to these natives, for such things have become necessary. It would be every bit as sane a policy to attempt to rid the Arctic Ocean of ice as to attempt to keep breech-loading arms from these natives. The introduction of fire-arms has greatly reduced the supply of game and driven most of the deer inland, for the natives often kill game now simply for the sport of shooting something.

The cutter is of inestimable service to the whalemen. Millions of dollars' worth of property and hundreds of lives are concerned. At any instant a part, or the whole, of the fleet may be jeopardized. Furthermore, the presence of the cutter has a wholesome effect on unruly crews, and it keeps harmony between the whalemen and the natives, and among the natives themselves. The physician is also in demand. By the aid of medical books a ship-master often proves a good nurse and physician. It so happened this year the forecastle of one of the steamers contained a physician whom drink had degraded. But the presence of the cutter's physician alone can be depended upon, and is a necessity when so many lives are at stake and the nearest port nearly two thousand miles off.

Russia makes a pretense to keep whisky and fire-arms out of the hands of the Masinkers, but it amounts to nothing. I was told by Indian Point natives that when the Russian man-of-war came north in 1886, several barrels of liquor were found in the settlement. These were left undisturbed, but what breech-loading rifles could be conveniently found were taken away from the natives. It would seem to the average mortal as if a rifle would be of more use in earning a living in this barren corner of the world than any amount of whisky. The

Eskimo have lost their cunning with the bow and arrow, spear, and other weapons of former days. To expect a return to the use of these is decidedly absurd.

After taking my letters on board the tender, I prepared to launch out in that terror of terrors, the Arctic Ocean. Steamer *Lucretia*, Capt. A. C. Sherman, was about to sail, so I transferred my traps, and by midnight we were in the Arctic Ocean.

Veins of coal crop out at various places along the northern coast of Alaska, between Cape Prince of Wales and Point Lay. The best veins are twenty miles or so above Cape Lisburne, which was our destination. The next morning—July 10th—we were far into the ocean. Occasionally, as the fog would lift, we could see the land at the south of us, otherwise there was only the vast expanse of the blue sea, with its slight, short swell. Not a sail or a cake of ice could be seen, nothing indicated that we were in any but an ordinary sea, yet my imagination urged me into the belief that there was something extraordinary in our surroundings; that we were tempting fate by being in a forbidden place. Visions of terrific gales

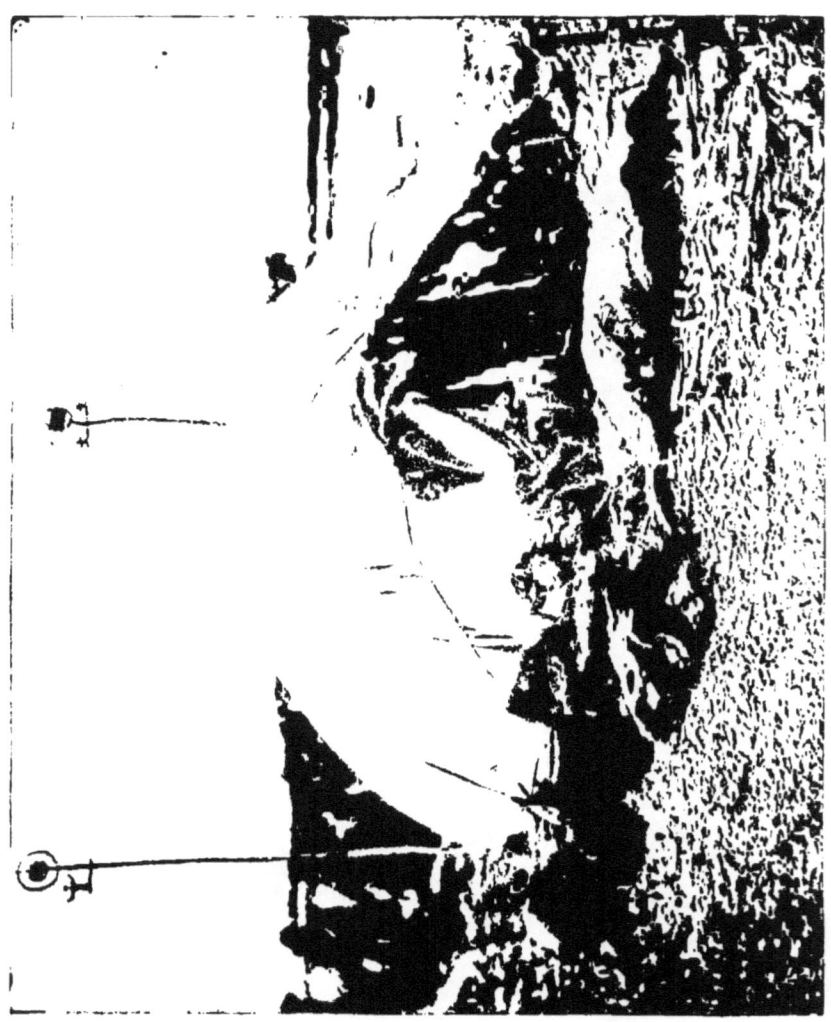

A MEDICINE MAN'S TOOTUCK—Page 85.
(The signs indicate that he doctors by the sun and the moon.)

and destructive ice-floes passed before me, yet we steamed on through a smooth, clear sea, without mishap or hindrance.

The next forenoon we anchored among a dozen or so vessels, that lay off Point Hope, waiting for the *Thomas Pope*, the tender to the New Bedford fleet. We had the mail from the *Bear*, and as the various captains came aboard in answer to the mail signal, we learned the good news that five more whales had been caught than were before reported, and the unpleasant news that the *Helen Mar* had been stove by ice, but not very seriously. One sailor, a consumptive, had died, and another had been killed by an accident. Two or three sailors had run away. The average sailor has a mania for running away, never mind how barren or desolate the place may be. If he can not run away, he wants to set fire to something. Or what he prefers to either of these, if it be in his power, is to get most thoroughly drunk. In a few days the runaways got satisfaction and returned.

As soon as the mail was distributed we hove up anchor and got under way for the coal mines, arriving there about seven o'clock in the evening. Cape Lisburne—so named by Captain Cook—kept up its old reputation for being a rough point to turn. Whenever the wind is southerly it seems to muster its strength under the bluff on the east side of the Cape—which is 850 feet high at its extremity—to be prepared to pounce down upon passing vessels and roll their keels up. We were working along with steam and fore-and-aft sails until the Cape was reached, and then we got it. The wind whistled and the ship responded by attempting to lie down sideways. For a moment it seemed as if the waves and the topmasts would embrace, but we forged ahead, righted up, and soon reached smooth sailing.

The tender appeared on the 14th. Twenty-five vessels were now riding at anchor, and as all were anxious to be moving on, times were busy night and day until each vessel had obtained her supply of vegetables, and stores, and shipped her whalebone. Letters had to be read and answered, and gossip exchanged. Four days later only four vessels remained.

As the ships began to scatter, the half dozen or so toopicks on the shore were struck, and the natives went on a big deer hunt. One family alone remained. In several trips ashore I had noticed a slight difference in appearance of these natives from those at Port Clarence. There, cloth was much used as under-clothing, hence fur garments were worn with the hair side out, and being made with some regard to taste, the result was often not unpicturesque. Here but little cloth was used, and clothing was generally worn with the fur side in. Most every frock— or, to use the native name, *artiggi*—had its hood here, but at Port Clarence this attachment was frequently omitted. Many women had a cloth gown that was short like an apron. Skirts that extended below the knee did not seem to be tolerated. One gown that I saw was made of a patchwork bed-quilt. It must have made a striking appearance before the gaudy colors were toned down and blended together with dirt.

Practically no trade was to be had here. A curious feature of trading with the Eskimo is the manner in which prices change. On one ship price enough will be offered by a sailor for an article to usually purchase much more, but without avail. Then this very article will be taken to another vessel and gladly exchanged for a fraction of what has just been offered for it. A "louse comb"—the significant name by which a fine comb is known in trade—will frequently purchase what that and a knife would not have bought half an hour before. The Eskimo never show all the trade they have, but carry a little here and a little there, perhaps producing something new every day, but always keeping something behind, mayhaps in anticipation of dull times and little trade the next season.

Flowers in large variety, and some exquisitely scented ones, grow here. Two familiar faces were the dandelion and the white daisy. The ubiquitous mosquito, with his large family, was also here. His fierce war-songs would occasionally be interspersed with a bass solo from the industrious bumble-bee. One day I found a bee on a dandelion blossom, while within a stone's throw was a snow-drift nearly two hundred feet deep. Besides flowers, this region abounds in geological specimens. The bluff is of trap-rock, crossed by frequent veins of coal, and in spots ferns of various sorts are found preserved in the rock. I found four distinct varieties.

I bought of one native a fancy bag made of

several kinds of fur and decorated with tips of red and blue yarn over white deer-skin. A narrow red strip was a part of the decorating, and at first glance I supposed it to be seal-skin tanned red. Instead, however, it proved to be a piece of an old flannel shirt. While wandering among the toopicks one day I came across several women skinning ducks for food, and I noticed that some of them would take an occasional bite of the raw flesh. At another time a canoe-load of natives, men, women, and children, made a meal of raw deer meat, scraping every bone as clean as though it were sandpapered. Such sights afterward became everyday occurrences, and the novelty soon wore off. It was after eating this venison that I noticed a young girl have an after-dinner smoke, then take her pipe to pieces and eat, with apparent relish, the nicotine that had collected in it.

We had on board a rooster, the last of a once large family, and he welcomed in each morning with a spell of vigorous crowing. This must have been from force of habit, for, as the sun did not set, as it was the middle of the period of the midnight sun he could not welcome its rising. The cliff would reverberate his efforts, and he would chase the echoes until near exhaustion.

The weather was warm and clear, so that work was not interrupted, and in the ten days that we lay here we mined ninety tons of coal. One warm afternoon, with the thermometer registering about 65°, several of us went in bathing in a pool at the mouth of one of the creeks. The air was chilly, but the water was warmer than I ever knew salt water to be on the New England sea-coast north of Cape Cod. The salt water was icy cold with many cakes of ice floating in it; but this small stream, coming down from the water-shed, a short distance off, got full benefit of the sun's warm rays. The earth was thawed out a foot or two. With this shallow soil and the short summer, the term of vegetation is only about fifty days.

The *Thomas Pope* sailed on the morning of the 20th, with a cargo equal in value to that of the other tender. Thirty-six hours later, our anchor was up and we were bound northward. With the tender went the last link that connected us with the world. There could be no communication to us, or from us, for over three months. We had "burned our ships behind us," and launched out into a region beset with dangers. The chances were one to fifteen that we would be wrecked. Hardly more than two hundred miles ahead of us were the scenes of the two great wreck seasons, when millions of dollars' worth of property had been destroyed and scores of lives sacrificed. Yet we pushed ahead, heedless of these things, in the hope of getting a goodly number of whales. What a delightful prospect for three months of enjoyment!

At Point Lay we found most of the sailing vessels. We remained with them a day or so, then pushed on again. The Sea Horse Islands, low sand-bars, were soon astern, and for ten hours we pushed ahead, occasionally dodging ice. Night set in with a heavy fog and suspicious movements in the ice caused by the strong current. The next morning—the 30th—prudence advised turning our backs on Point Barrow—our objective point—and retreating. This we did, but it was a narrow escape, the most serious predicament I had been in. The fog was intensely thick, so that no course could be laid out. The ice was heavy, and moving off to the northeast at a rapid rate. An occasional "toot" at the whistle would be answered by the other steamers within hearing. We thus kept track of each other and prevented collision. We struck a cake of ice so hard that we supposed we were stove. The danger signal —three whistles— was sounded, only to be answered by another steamer in a like predicament. For six hours we wormed along through the ice under full head of steam, yet we did not accomplish over twenty miles, though we were steaming at the rate of six miles. At last we emerged into clear water.

Since leaving the coal mines we had seen only a low shore. There are a few small bluffs, but for the most part the shore is low, marshy, and broken by lagoons. Consequently ships keep well off. Wainwright Inlet hardly exceeds a fathom in depth. At Point Belcher the land is a trifle higher, and it is crowned by a large settlement. Only three toopicks were seen there, showing that the most of the inhabitants were off trading or hunting. The scene of the great wreck of 1871 was solid with ice and we passed considerably off shore from it.

THE SUN AT MIDNIGHT.—Page 85.

On the afternoon of August 2d we dropped anchor opposite the settlement at Cape Smyth, seven miles below Point Barrow.

CHAPTER IV.

WHALING.

Though many whales were caught by the ships in Behring Sea, I did not happen to be near enough to enjoy the sport, and it was not until we anchored under East Cape that I saw my first whale caught. Everything had been so interesting, however, that I had not been disappointed, and after I had seen the first one, I rejoiced that it was the first, everything was so favorable. The day was beautiful, and the captain and I embraced the opportunity to make the round of the nine ships at anchor and relate the story of the wrecked man at Cape Navarin. When on the extreme northern ship, a whale was "raised," or seen, coming leisurely along up the edge of the shore-ice. The news spread like wild-fire, and in a few minutes thirty or more whale-boats were flitting about, each endeavoring to get as near as possible to the spot where the whale would next rise to spout.

When he rose a boat darted an iron, but it did not hold. At the next rising another boat attempted to hit him, but also failed; but the third boat made fast to him. It was a grand sight to see the whale make a lunge and start seaward, towing the boat after him at a terrific pace. He went a mile or two, then wheeled about and made a straight line for the shore-ice. Another boat was soon along-side to bend on more line to the nearly exhausted tubs of the fast boat.

All the captains became so excited and interested in the chase that they longed for some of the fun, so four of them took the Hunter's steam-launch, I accompanying them. As soon as we reached the shore ice I saw the whale spout behind a long point of ice. It would have taken a boat considerable time to sail there, but we steamed around it, and before I could comprehend the situation, were alongside the monster. It seemed incredible that such a powerful creature could be killed. With Captain Cogan at the helm, Captain Sherman with a darting-gun, Captain Kelley with a shoulder-gun, and Captain Winslow and me as ballast, we bore down on him, fired two bombs into him, and rushed past just in time to escape a sweeping blow from his powerful tail.

It is disappointing to see a whale, for most pictures represent him as standing up like a buoy or posing on his tail on top of the water. The real fact is that only the top of the head about the spout-hole, and a small piece of the back, are seen, and perhaps the "flukes," or

A WHALEBOAT AND A WHALE COMPARED IN SIZE.

in common English, the tail, may take an occasional sweep in the air. When, as near as we were, so that we could look down into the water upon the creature, his great size could be partially comprehended.

It seems to be the duty of every man in the boat when the whale is struck, to yell at the top of his voice. Even where there is dignity to be kept up, a certain amount of this has to be done. In the midst of the shouting was heard the muffled "boom," "boom" of the two bombs, and the whale rolled over, dead, without a struggle. I stayed aboard the Lucretia that night to see the whale cut-in.

As soon as a whale is killed the vessel gets under way, and sails to him, taking him on the starboard side, in front of the gangway. With a steamer, as in this instance, this is very easily done, but a sailing-vessel may find it necessary to maneuver some time before getting the conditions right for work. First a strong chain, or hawser, is secured around the flukes. This runs through the hawse-pipe and is firmly fastened to the forward bit near the windlass. Then another chain is secured to one fin, and it is with this second chain that the whale is managed.

The carcass runs fore-and-aft, the head being aft, and the fin in front of the gangway. With sharp cutting spades, a man cuts through the blubber, circling around the whale from the extremity of the mouth toward the tail, corkscrew like. He cuts down to the "lean." By hauling on the fin-chain the carcass rolls, and the "blanket-piece" of blubber tears itself off, aided by the cutting spades. When the whale is rolled quarter over one lip comes uppermost. A tackle is fastened to this; then it is cut off, hoisted on deck and dropped into the "blubber room," as the space between decks, from the mainmast to the forecastle, is called. All hoisting is done by the windlass, and in most of the vessels power comes from a donkey-engine. The blanket-piece is started again and the whale rolled half-way over. The throat is then uppermost. This in turn is cut off, and deposited in the blubber room, then the other lip is rolled up and removed. By this time the blanket-piece becomes unwieldy in its length, so another hold is secured close down to the carcass, and the strip of blubber, perhaps fifteen feet long and six feet wide, cut off and dropped into the blubber room.

The most difficult part of the whole operation is now at hand, and that is to cut off the "head," or upper jaw, which contains all the whalebone. A false or careless move might destroy hundreds of dollars worth of bone, or, possibly, cause the loss of the whole head. A chain is carefully drawn through a hole cut between the scalp bone and the tough blubber about the spout-hole. The backbone is chopped nearly through, near where the blanket-piece was started, then by a jerk of the tackle the weight breaks the remainder and the head is hauled on deck. There was once a whaling captain who disjointed the head instead of chopping it off. This whale's head contained about twenty-five hundred pounds of whalebone, and as the price of bone was three dollars and fifty cents a pound at that time, it can readily be seen how anxious a whaleman must be, when cutting-in, until he gets the head on deck. Heads contain over six hundred slabs of bone, and in a large whale like this, the pieces range in length from twelve feet, or a little over, down to a few inches. For convenience in working, each ship has a "cutting stage" of planks that hangs over the water in front of the gangway, so that the men can stand nearly over the whale. It is from this that the work is done, and it was here that I stood to see the whole operation.

With the head cut off, the rest of the cutting-in is easy and simple. The blanket piece is peeled off in strips about fifteen feet long, until a point near the flukes is reached. There the backbone is disjointed. The final haul brings on deck the flukes with the blanket-piece. The carcass either floats off or sinks. These blanket-pieces of blubber are cut and torn off the whale in the same manner that the peel is cut and torn off an orange when paring it. Frequently the natives are aboard, and work is done slowly in order that they may have an opportunity to cut off as much as possible of the lean meat. The cutting-in was a novelty to me, but the work of the natives was more entertaining. They had six canoes crowded in near the whale, and the instant there was a lull in the proceedings, a man from each would clamber on to the carcass, splash about in the blood and water, and slash away at the meat with villainous looking knives. They worked like heroes and yelled like fiends. Some worked with their hands under water, and most of them were knee-deep in it all the time. One fellow lay almost flat on his stomach and burrowed in under the blubber in advance of the cutters. His feet were flying about dangerously near keen-edged knives, but he did not get cut.

Whalemen still observe the old sperm-whaling custom of lustily shouting "Hurrah for

THE MISSING LINK — A POINT LAY NATIVE. Page 87.

five and forty more" when the head or last piece of blubber is landed on deck. But this shout is not because the work is all done.

TENDING THE TRY-POTS.

Early the next morning the try-pots were set to working. First, the blubber was cut into "horse pieces" about a foot square and two feet long, then "minced," that is, cut into thin slices to facilitate the trying-out of the oil. The blubber then goes into the pots, and after the oil is boiled out, the remains of the blubber have become hard and brittle, but are pressed to get the last dregs of oil; then these "scraps" are used for fuel, and they make a hot fire. This night the sun barely dipped below the horizon at midnight, but when darkness does interfere with the cutting-in, or the trying-out, a lot of scraps are put into a wire basket and lighted, making a "bug light" which is equal to a pitch pine torch. The oil is slowly bailed from the try-pots into a cooler, and after running through two or three, is pumped into casks and stowed down in the hold. This whale made one hundred and twenty barrels of oil.

Such a feast as the natives had after their work was finished! They scattered all over the ship, and in their canoes, eating blubber. Each one was gnawing away on a big chunk, sometimes of several pounds. He would surround one corner with his mouth, grasp it in his teeth, then saw it off with his knife. Why the lips were not sawed off was a mystery. The bigger the mouthful the more happy he appeared.

Whenever opportunity offered, whether while gamming, or at other times, I asked the various captains how much a hundred-barrel whale would weigh. Some estimated it at thirty tons, others forty or fifty, and not a few were as high as seventy-five tons. Even a "calf," as the young whale is called, that is only four days old, is a heavy load to haul on deck. With polar whales the "cow," or female, is larger than the "bull," or male. With all other species of whales it is just the other way.*

Our next whaling was off Point Barrow. When we left Cape Smyth we steamed around the ground-ice along the shore into the open water beyond.

Two other steamers were in sight whaling, and soon we, too, had boats down. Two whales were disporting themselves on the edge of the

---

* The following are the measurements of a whale eighty barrels in size, made by Captain J. F. Poole, of the *N. S. Perkins*, of San Francisco, in August, 1867: Total length, forty-seven feet; length of pectorals, or "fins," eight feet; breadth of pectorals, four feet; distance from nib end to spout-holes, sixteen feet ten inches; extension of the flukes, nineteen feet; thickest part of blubber, one foot four inches; thickness of the black skin, one inch; length of the longest piece of whalebone, eleven feet one inch; distance the bone was imbedded in the gum of the jaw, ten inches; number of pieces of whalebone on each side, 330; weight of the longest piece of whalebone, seven pounds.

ice just ahead of the ship, and a boat made fast to one of them, but lost him. Two hours later another whale was struck and lost; but not long afterward a third was struck, killed, and secured. When struck, he darted under the ice, taking nearly all the line in the boat, but the bombs

BOATS OFF CRUISING.

had done their fatal work. Slowly and carefully he was hauled out, and when once alongside, was quickly cut in. Boats were off cruising along the edge of the ice most of the time. During two nights young ice formed, so no whaling was done. One evening a large whale came up astern of the ship, about three ship-lengths off, spouted three or four times, then disappeared under the ice. He took so little time and was so spry, that a boat was not lowered quick enough. Even my detective camera seemed to work slow, but I "shot" in time to get him as he rounded to go down.

We were in a narrow channel between the ground-ice at the south and the main pack at the north. The current ran through this like a mill-stream. In it a sailing-vessel would be perfectly helpless. Even the steamers found it no easy task to make headway against it. This powerful current, with a northeasterly trend, has carried many a ship to destruction. There was more or less change in the pack every day, usually according to the direction of the wind. Once it nearly closed in on us, driving out some of the steamers. When the second change came we all got out as fast as sail and steam could carry us. No vessel can be built that could withstand being nipped between ice, grounded so as to brace itself on the one side, and the pack with millions upon millions of tons pressing behind it on the other side.

For six weeks we lay around Point Barrow. Whenever the ice would allow of it, we would go out along the edge of the pack, or floe, and hunt for whales. Frequently we would pick up one or two, but more often the ice would drive us back to our retreat before we could begin whaling. But no time was lost when whaling was possible. The ship's crew was divided into "watches." One watch would be on deck eight hours one night and four hours the following day, while the other watch would have the eight hours for rest—the "watch below," and the four hours for the "watch on deck." By alternating, one watch would sleep most of one night, then be on deck most of the next night. But there was no regard either for the watch below or the watch on deck, when there was whaling to be done. There are very few days in the eight months' cruise when whaling can be done, so no opportunity is lost, be it Sunday or any other time.

The old way of whaling, simply with harpoons and lances, has long since been superseded by the use of bombs. The bombs contain nearly a pound of powerful powder, and when they explode inside of a whale, shatter it mercilessly. They are shot from a heavy metallic shoulder-gun, or from a "darting gun." This is a gun attached to a pole about six feet long. A harpoon is fitted to the gun, so the operation of "darting" the harpoon is like the old method. But when the harpoon, or "iron," is "made fast" to the whale, the bomb is shot from the gun. It enters the whale's body and explodes in a few seconds, usually in a vital spot, and kills the whale instantly, hence the royal sport that whaling was under the harpoon system, has now become merely a butchering operation. There are cases, however, when a whale shows great fight. Sperm whales are born fighters, but polar whales are timid and die meekly.

We found one whale that was not meek. When off in the ice, in a large hole some two miles in diameter, we struck a whale that spouted thick blood. This was an indication of a fatal wound, but he seemed determined to die game. Heading for the middle of the hole, he swept his flukes through the air, smashing the rudder of one boat, then plunging ahead in his terrible agony. His huge head would come out of the water, then his flukes would take a sweep in the air. Five boats were about him, each endeavoring to put another bomb into him, and yet not get within reach of his destructive tail. Once he headed for the pack, but we steamed in front of him and headed him off. Then, at a favorable opportunity, a boat ran up to him. The boat-steerer raised his gun, and was about to shoot, when the whale disappeared. Again he came up, made another exhibition of his giant strength, and sank. For a quarter of an hour we watched him poking his head out of the water, swinging his huge flukes about, and making faint attempts to spout.

Trailing on quietly and calmly behind him, all this time, were two frail cedar whale-boats, each made fast to him by a small steel harpoon and a hempen line two inches in circumference. With each rising he seemed to gain additional strength, but the boats followed closer than he could guard against. At last, a good shot was had. The muffled report of its explosion followed, and he rolled over, dead. "Hurrah!" shouted every man in the boats and on the ship. It was a shout of victory, a victory of human skill and cunning over nature's royal brute, the embodiment of strength and bigness. Few men in the crew had ever witnessed such a spectacle before. Certainly I never had, and never expect to again. It was a victory worthy

STARTING THE BLANKET-PIECE.—Page 9.

the superior intelligence of man. To come upon a whale and kill him instantly is a tame affair, but to defy him to combat, circumvent him at every point, and finally kill him, is entirely a different thing.

On the morning of the next day the boats were off whaling, and I was watching them, when the lookout said, "See there!" A large polar bear with one cub was wandering along the edge of the pack, climbing over one hummock after another until they got within two ship-lengths of us. There they halted, for they saw the ship, but being at the windward could not scent it. Their noses were high in the air sniffing, and as they patiently held them there, I took the hint and photographed them. The scene was exceedingly interesting, for they were the first bears I had seen, but it was rudely intruded upon by somebody calling out "Fast boat!" In an instant, two white, shaggy creatures were seen to head about and scamper away as fast as their clumsiness could carry them. No bullet followed them, but my camera caught them as they were disappearing over a hummock. Before noon, we had a hundred-and-twenty-barrel whale cut in.

The food of the bowhead-whale is found in "slicks," and these slicks give to the water the appearance of oily streaks. The different kinds of jelly-fish that cause these slicks are "bird's-eye," "snow-flake," "sun-gall," etc. They range from the size of a pea, in the first named, to six inches or more in diameter, as is the case with the sun-gall. This last is found on the Atlantic Coast, and sometimes in New York harbor. Bowheads also eat red shrimp, young salmon, and other young fish. All whales are fat or lean according to the supply of feed. The whalebone is all in the upper jaw, while the lower jaw has two large lips, one on each side. Whalebone is covered on the inner edge with coarse hair, like horse-hair, which also covers the roof of the mouth. When feeding, the whale spreads out his broad lips, swims rapidly through a feed-slick, and when his mouth is full of the food-charged water, he closes the lips partly, then forces the water out of his mouth with his tongue. The hair serves as a sieve and collects all the feed. This is swallowed, and then the operation is repeated until his appetite is satiated.

While at anchor one day, I looked over the

ship's books to see how much we ate, and I found that our eight month's supply of food was 60 barrels of flour; 4,000 pounds of ship-bread; 70 barrels of salt beef and pork; 100 pounds of salt cod-fish; 400 bushels of potatoes; 1,000 pounds of sugar; 300 gallons of molasses; 1,000 pounds of coffee; 150 pounds of tea; 1,000 or more cans of meat, vegetables, fruit, etc., besides small groceries.

The men are paid a percentage, or "lay," the lay being "long" or "short" according to the ability or position of the man. The captain gets the "shortest" lay, which varies from one-eighth of the total value of the voyage to a sixteenth. Then come the officers and the men, the lays growing "longer" down the list until the steerage-boy is reached, and he is fortunate if he gets a two-hundredth. Each ship has five whale-boats, and these boats are in charge of the officers and the boat-headers, the captain always being in the crow's nest to direct the boats by a code of signals. While the boat-header—for each officer is a boat-header—manages and steers the boat, the boat-steerer uses the harpoon, and frequently also the shoulder-gun. Boats always sail down to the whale. To use a paddle, or an oar, would frighten the whale the instant it touched the water. Each boat has two hundred fathoms of line coiled in tubs, which is used with the harpoon. Then, as emergency articles, there is a keg of fresh water, a keg of bread, a lantern, and an ax to chop the line in case the whale threatens to swamp the boat.

Whale-ships are naturally oily, though they are thoroughly scrubbed with lye after the whaling is over. This oilyness has saved many a whaler from wreck. A good illustration of this is the experience of Capt. Edward Penniman when he was master of the *Minerva*. His was one of the last ships to leave the Arctic, having fallen in with many whales. When he had the blubber of several on board, he headed out, keeping the try-works running. Soon a severe gale came on; the blubber all shifted to one side, giving the ship a bad list, and making her unmanageable; the weather was too thick to see anything, and she drifted into the breakers on the shoals off Cape Prince of Wales. One heavy sea after another broke over her, threatening destruction to everything on board, for she was on her beam ends with her lee rail under water. But one very heavy sea stove several casks of oil that were on deck. Like magic the sea stopped breaking; the captain wore ship, reached deep water, and escaped.

On September 6th I changed to the steamer *Beluga*, Capt. J. F. Brooks. That afternoon the northeast current was the strongest I had yet seen it, and as the day was very calm, several sailing-vessels were entirely at its mercy, slowly but surely bound to their destruction. But happily the close of the day brought a breeze, and they escaped. That night we anchored along the ground-ice off Cape Smyth, where there were a dozen or more sailing-vessels that had just come up. Almost the first news that we heard was that the revenue cutter had been successful in the search at Cape Navarin, and rescued Vincent.

Scarcely a day passed without more or less mirage, and at times the effect was marvelous. Ships would be reflected long before they hove in sight, or perhaps the ice would be piled up in fantastic walls or masses. The horizon would be irregular on account of this, and remain so for hours, there being practically no tide. The highest tide is three feet, but the average for the year is only about ten inches.

A whaling and trading station has been maintained for some years in the building erected just above Cape Smyth, by the United States Government, for the Signal Service Expedition under Lieutenant Ray in 1880-2; with a small sloop and two boats' crews, whaling is carried on whenever the weather and the ice permit, and the whales are agreeable. Whalebone and furs are also traded for with the natives. The presence of the station has probably saved the lives of many natives by furnishing food in exchange for work. The average native is the most improvident being imaginable. He can not have regard for the future. His desire to trade amounts almost to a mania. He will trade off his last bit of ammunition, or remnant of food, seemingly for the sake of trading; the case is not as infrequent as it might be in which he will trade off his own child. Death by starvation is as frequent as death from natural causes, but it would be much less frequent were he more provident and energetic. At the station a large supply of venison is always on hand and no more toothsome steaks can be imagined than I ate there.

Two days at the anchorage and we were off again, the wind having scattered the edge of the pack. A strong northwesterly gale coming on, we could not safely move, the ice was changing about so much. But we were under a lee of ground-ice, so were secure. Soon that began to break up and threaten damage to the sailing-vessels. In fact, two of them were driven ashore. Some retreated down the coast, but half a dozen of the bolder ones pushed ahead and anchored behind the Point. In spite of the gale, we went off toward the pack next morning. It was the only direction we could go in, for the pack had swung around on the land at the south, cutting off retreat, and it would not have been an impossible condition of affairs for it to have remained so for the rest of the season. A few days later, however, a change in the wind scattered the ice.

When the whales enter the Arctic, they follow up the American shore into the northeast as fast as the ice breaks up. They go—nobody knows where, but it is surmised, into the great basin at the mouth of the Mackenzie river. But the eastward of Point Barrow is a dangerous region; there may not be a cake of ice in sight, yet a sudden change in the wind may bring up the pack in a twinkling. No places of retreat are at hand, for the water is shallow inshore, hence ships, if caught, would be most likely pushed high and dry on the beach. Ships of much draught drag their keels in the mud if they go far to the eastward. One of the greatest dangers in Arctic whaling is this going east of Point Barrow. Yet the steamers and many sailing-vessels venture there at every opportunity. Franklin's Return Reef is the farthest limit, though in 1886, steamers reached Barter Island, and aimed at Herschel's Island, four hundred and fifty miles from Point Barrow. Had they gone there, however, they would have been shut in for the winter. We went fifty miles to the eastward, when the sudden change in the wind caused us to have an anxiety to see what was behind us. Some of the boats were off cruising, and before they could be called aboard they were caught. By hauling over the ice, however, they finally got aboard, but not before one had been badly stove. Returning to the Point, we found the whole fleet, with but two or three

FIG. 16.—GETTING OFF A DIP.

vessels lacking, at anchor. The next morning an off-shore gale greeted us. This gale drove all the ground-ice out, and two days afterward hardly a cake was to be seen. Meantime I had moved to the *Wanderer*, Capt. S. P. Smith. The steamers again disappeared into the eastward, and as the weather permitted, some sailing-vessels followed. Others squared their yards and headed westward. Twelve or fifteen of us felt our way around in the fog for six days, part of the time at anchor, and nearly all the time blowing a fog-horn.

One stray whale was picked up, but whaling was so "dry" that the other vessels now squared away also for the westward.

CHAPTER V.

POINT BARROW, HOME.

Midway between Point Barrow and Cape Smyth is the "Shooting Station," a favorite rendezvous for duck hunters. While on the *Grampus*, Capt. Henry G. Dexter, we were forced to anchor off this Station. I went ashore, and while there, saw sad effects of the pernicious habit of treating, to which Americans are so wedded. Over half the adult natives, regardless of sex, were intoxicated. Some of the men were paralyzed with liquor, and one old fellow was frothing at the mouth in his crazy delirium. He understood the use of liquor well, for the next day he kicked his wife to death. From personal observation, I knew that over half the fifteen or so toopicks had their victims. A little *long-a*—liquor—would have purchased the whole settlement and everything in it. In fact, no trade but that would be taken. Liquor is not directly traded, but now and then a captain, in his insatiate desire to make a few dollars, shows the quality of his character by lubricating a bargain for whalebone with a few drinks of whisky, and perhaps makes a present of a bottle or so to the unfortunate possessor of the bone. Such cases are few, but they should be fewer, and the captain of the cutter neglects his duty in not making them fewer. Most whalemen refuse to trade liquor, or treat with it, under any consideration. But in every walk of life it is not impossible to find a man who will jump at an opportunity to sell himself to the devil for money. The ships that sold the liquor had taken their trade and disappeared to conceal their deviltry.

Snow-squalls soon became frequent, and young ice formed every night. Our supply of fresh water was not sufficient to carry the season through, and as plenty was to be had on a large cake near by, we tied up to it and pumped sixty or seventy barrels into our tanks. Double that amount could have been easily obtained. The warm rays of the sun in summer melt the snow and ice on the floes, and form basins of fresh water. If the ice be low and flat, the water gets salty, but on cakes like this one, high above the salt water line, the water is very good.

During the winter of 1876-7, a jam off the Point left a mountain of ice that towered far above the masts of the ships, and remained for two years. This was the biggest ice whalemen have ever seen here, ice at other times being "big" that is half as high as the masts. The past winter had been free from gales, hence no jams had occurred, and all the ice was comparatively low and flat.

August 31st I went on board the steamer *Thrasher*, Capt. Charles E. Weeks. Bad weather kept all the steamers at anchor for the week following. This gave me opportunity to go ashore. For some minutes I stood on the extreme northern point of the continent, so close to the water that an occasional ripple would wet my boot. The beach was covered with ice. As far as the eye could reach into the north and eastward, was ice, blue in its solidity, and no more penetrable than so much granite. To the westward was our only avenue of retreat, and that was apparently solid with ice for two or three miles off shore, and then there was

only a narrow open space of clear water between
that and the solid north pack. A strong current coming out from the lagoon behind the
Point swept a clear path just off the shore from
the eastern pack to the ice at the north. Looking east, north, or west, there seemed to be
nothing but ice—a monotonous and chilly
prospect. What was beyond, even the imagination could not surmise. Half a mile back
from the Point was the settlement, where generation after generation of Eskimo have lived
and died, yet each and all have looked with
awe and dread upon the great unknown region
at the north. As I turned to go to the settlement, I picked up a few pebbles, one of
which was half under water, yet the particle
of the continent that was farthest north.

Point Barrow is low and sandy, but half a
mile back it rises to a height of perhaps fifty
feet above the sea, and on this bluff is the settlement. The most northern building is a rude
wooden structure, which I was told was a dance-hall. Scattered among the igaloos were a dozen
or so toopicks. A greater part of the inhabitants were away; of the few that were at home,
old people and invalids seemed to be in the

majority. It was pitiable to see some of them. One poor woman had frozen both feet, and mortification had set in, causing much of the flesh to fall off nearly to her knees. Another was afflicted with a large running sore. An old man, with some organic difficulty, could not leave his toopick. In these, and other like cases, we were asked for medicine. The poor creatures, entirely at the mercy of disease, were dirty, squalid, ignorant, and helpless. None of the igaloos were occupied, but in some cases the work of preparing them for the coming winter was going on. Sods and cakes of peat were being dug in a marsh near by, and placed over windholes and wherever else was necessary.

Some igaloos had their entrances blocked up by stagnant water; others had water inside, possibly having been permanently deserted. In all cases, the windows were broken and covered with boards, cloth, or the like. Finding one large igaloo that was dry, I took the liberty to drop down through the window into it. This was the most northern habitation on the continent, which added to my desire to see it. The roof was high, so that I could stand erect. Across the north end of the room was a platform, raised about a yard from the floor and extending out from the wall five feet. A bundle of deer skins neatly rolled up lay on it; underneath were a box and one or two household utensils. Close to the wall on the south side was an oval hole in the floor large enough for one not very corpulent, to crawl through; this lead to the entrance proper. A few cooking and other utensils stood in a corner near by; in the other corner was a small blubber-oil "stove." On each side of the room was another of these stoves; each was made of a piece of three-inch plank, probably wreckage. The first one was about eighteen inches long, the second about two feet, and the third three feet. They were hollowed out to a depth of an inch and a half, and raised slightly from the floor. There was no moss on them to serve as a wick, nor oil in them, but a piece of well-smoked blubber hung nearly two feet above each, indicating that they had seen service. The walls were of smooth boards closely held together, and the floor was a good one. Everything was as scrupulously neat, clean, and orderly, as any housekeeper could wish for. The three lamps were thickly coated with grease, but that could not be otherwise. Every article seemed to have its own place and be in it, three or four racks on the walls containing many of the smaller articles. The size of this igaloo was twelve by fourteen feet. Outside, opposite the entrance, was the usual staging or scaffold, on which were some whalebone, perhaps fifty pounds, deerskins, a bear, and other skins, two dead seals, and other valuables. Evidently the owner of the place was in good circumstances.

After seeing the place of the living, I went to "Dead Man's Island" to see the place of the dead. It is a low sand-heap half a mile long and not ten feet above the sea-level at its highest point. There were evidences of perhaps thirty graves, but not over half a dozen were intact. The rest were marked by a collection of a few bones, most of the skeletons being scattered in all directions. Respect for the dead does not seem to exist in the average Eskimo. If one dies who has no property or family influence, a team of dogs is harnessed to his corpse, and he is dragged to the outskirts of the settlement and abandoned to the mercy of the village canines. They promptly despoil it of all flesh. If, however, there be property or influence, the body, with

A HEAD OF WHALEBONE. Page 95.

most of the personal effects, is wrapped in a piece of canvas, or in skins, and deposited among other like dead. This particular place of the dead happened to be beyond the reach of the dogs, but others that I saw were not. As the Eskimo dog is no respecter of corpses, the ultimate result is always the same, regardless of what the worldly condition of the deceased may have been.

The morning of the 7th dawned clear, and everybody was promptly under way. The easterly gale had broken up and scattered the ice. Then followed a week of fine weather, and we succeeded in catching several whales off near the pack. The afternoon of the 13th day of September was rainy, and it continued to drizzle well through the night. A week before we had lain under the Point, nearly hedged in by the ice, and surrounded by every indication of the approach of winter, young ice formed nightly, and the land was white with snow. Now we were experiencing a midsummer, temperate-zone rain. But Arctic weather is fickle, as shown by the records of the previous spring as kept at the whaling station. On March 23d it was 14° below zero at 7 A. M., and 36°

above in the evening; on the 25th it was 12° below at 7 A. M., 35° at noon, and 9° above at night; on the 28th the weather ranged from 30° below to 14° above. Such violent changes are particularly frequent during the first half of the year.

After this we saw no more whales, though we cruised for two days. It was evident that the Point Barrow whaling was over. To remain longer was to get caught in the young ice. As the whales leave Point Barrow they follow the edge of the pack, and are found all along its edge, even as far west as Herald Island.

On the 16th we headed westward. Leaving the vicinity of the Point, we steamed out to the pack, working with fore-and-aft sails. After steady work for an hour or two, we concluded that the strong northeast current, aided by a head wind, was carrying us astern. To buck against this combination would be too great a drain on the small coal pile, which was very precious, so we returned to the Point, and made use of the pleasant weather to test the chronometers, which had seen no service since April. The next day all but three steamers were bound west, aided by the wind, which was now fair.

That afternoon I moved for the last time, going to the steamer *Orca*, Capt. George F. Bauldry. The next morning the three remaining steamers were bound westward, and Point Barrow had seen her last ship until the next summer.

The edge of the pack was ragged and very irregular. Long points of ice were frequent, with occasional deep guts, or bights between them. Had we followed the straightest course possible, it would not have been long before we would have been in the vicinity of Herald Island. But instead, we skirted the edge of the pack, making our course very tortuous. Then for two days, or so, we had the strong northeast current against us. During the day-time we made progress, but at night we lay hove-to and the current consumed considerable of the day's headway.

Just two months before, I was photographing the sun at midnight. Now the sun did not rise early enough to be present at our six o'clock breakfasts. Then, too, it shortened up its hours proportionately at the other end of the day, so that it was quite dark at seven o'clock, and the hours for whaling were few.

Not a day passed but what we saw whales,

some in the ice, others in clear water. Occasionally one of the latter would be still, sunning himself, perhaps, as he lazily spouted and rolled with the swell, but he managed to keep his weather eye on the ships. The others went as though intrusted with some important message which required immediate delivery at a distant point. A favorite resort for the whales seemed to be in the porridge ice, fringing the pack. The heavy swell rubbed, rolled, and jumbled the scattering ice together, making porridge that was too much for a whaleboat to live in.

In about the longitude of $69\frac{1}{2}°$, and west latitude 169°, is always a long point of ice, caused, probably, by the peculiarities of the currents, and possibly backed up by shoal water. It was here that ships from the eastward and westward used to meet in former days and exchange news, hence it got to be called "Post-office Point." After passing this we raised a sail, then another, and another, and from this time on we were among the fleet again. Some vessels were boiling and we saw others get whales. Just ahead of us was the *Thrasher*, and she picked up a "stinker," as a dead whale is technically, and aptly, called. We passed within a mile of her, and it was near enough. Up to this time I had been regretting that I had not seen one of these dead whales, and been able to photograph it. Now, however, the gentle breezes that were wafted toward us from that direction laid their burdens directly under our noses, and from that moment I feared that one might make its appearance especially for my benefit.

We spoke several vessels, and nothing but good news was heard, except that one ship was reported still "clean," that is, without oil. Many vessels that left Point Barrow a month before, discouraged and disgusted, now had several whales apiece. In fact, a good season's work had already been done. The weather had been, and still was, perfect. Day after day we had enjoyed typical New England October days. Fog had not concealed the whales or embarrassed the vessels. Neither had gales interfered by scattering the ice and destroying shipping and whaling gear.

Whalemen usually count upon finding still whales in the waters about Herald Island, and as only four more were wanted to fill all our oil-tanks, we had hoped to find them there, but our cruising was in vain, so we returned eastward.

In rare instances whales are caught napping. I heard of two such cases this year. When the *Mary and Susan* was in the vicinity of the Sea-horse Islands, Captain Owen saw two still whales that were evidently asleep. The boats were off cruising at the time, but were called back, and one of them signaled on to these whales. Had two boats been there, both whales could easily have been killed, but as it was, only one was secured The other instance was with one of the *Orca's* boats. A whale lay asleep in a small hole in the ice. His breathing could be heard, but fearing to gally him by going over the ice, chase was given to another whale. Losing that, the boat returned and still heard the sleeper breathe. Going around the cake, a small lead wide enough for a boat to enter was found. In this little retreat the whale was sleeping in apparent contentment and security, when three bomb-lances were put into him. A spasmodic movement of the flukes was the only indication that the huge carcass had possessed life.

At the dawn of day on the 27th, whales were raised. A cold northerly wind was blowing, and a heavy swell was on, but this did not deter the boats from giving chase. When they returned, they were covered with ice. Whereever a drop of water struck, it had been instantly transformed into ice. The men, the boats, and the gear were heavily coated with it. The last blanket-piece was hauled on deck none too soon, for the wind rapidly increased to a gale. That night, and the next day, were rough enough, and cold enough, to satisfy any old sailor. In breaking, the waves threw water over the ship from stem to stern. The main deck was six inches or more deep with slush formed from the frozen spray, and the quarter-deck was but a little better off. In fact, everything that was exposed got its coating of ice. All around the hull, from the water-line to the rail, was a solid coating of ice, in some places a foot or more thick. The lower rigging was completely ice-bound. After forty-eight hours, pleasant weather appeared again, the wind became less furious, and the sea settled down to its usual moderate swell. The cold, however, abated but little after this. The sun's rays gradually cracked off our supercargo of ice, but they had no influence with the thermometer, which varied from 10° to 15° above zero, but with the atmosphere so humid, this was colder than 10° below zero in New England. Clear weather again was keenly appreciated, with its sparkling and crisp air. One could not but feel more buoyant and spirited, especially with the recent gale as a background.

It was on such mornings as these that Jack Frost exhibited his most artistic work. No more exquisite sight can be conceived than a ship, hull, rigging, and all, covered with a heavy coat of hoar-frost. What was black and dingy, became sparkling and bright. Heaviness and clumsiness became graceful and airy. The fancy depicts phantom ships as artistic and beautiful. But here is the stern reality of life, in the ruggedness of the Arctic Ocean, fairly bearding Boreas in his den, was something more than a phantom ship: a ship that combined all the strength and durability that genius and labor can command. It was not graceful or light, but clumsy, heavy, and devoid of everything ornamental or artistic. Yet when enshrouded by the hoar-frost with its own

A BANKED EDGE. Pl. 30.

spirit of beauty, the transformation was complete. The one is a fleeting dream that pleases the imagination; the other, an actuality that leaves a vivid imprint on the memory of its exquisite beauty

It is on such mornings, too, that the sailor hugs his seal or deer skin coat about him as the order comes to "lower away." With our four last whales the water was rugged, and the boats ploughed through, and sometimes under, the waves before conquering their prey. Woolen clothing would absorb water, and be frozen stiff in a few minutes in any of the boats, but the skins shed the water, and are only stiffened by the outside coating of ice. This was particularly true with next to the last whale. The gun was so iced up that it refused duty, hence the boat was fast to the whale with a harpoon, but with no bomb to explode. The whale towed the boat through and under many heavy seas; then took all the line. Other boats soon came up, and made an end to the struggle, but not before every man in the four boats had an ice overcoat on. When the men came on board and took their coats off, they fairly stood alone, being so stiffened with ice.

Such gales as the one just experienced are apt to drive off the ships, so that when the blow is over, they find themselves far from where the whales are. We had endeavored to hold on to the ice by steaming, but the wind drove us back to Herald Island. When we got eastward again to where the whales were, the cold interfered by causing much "smoke" to rise from the water. The air being many degrees colder than the water, caused condensation, and so much of this steam rose that the spoutings of the whales were obscured. Later, as the water grew colder, it became milky from this condensation, and less smoke arose. The wind drove the ice south, and as we lay aback nights, it drifted as fast as we did; thus we kept where the whales were.

At daylight on the morning of October 2d, the *Thrasher* was beheld with all colors out, a sign that she was "full." Her last whale was along-side, being cut in. About noon, she made all sail, and headed homeward, reporting tanks, casks, and everything full of oil, with twenty-five heads of bone. But the *Thrasher* was not alone in her proud display of colors, for before noon we had the twenty-eighth whale along-side. All the colors were run up, and, as the last blanket-piece came on deck, all hands set up a joyous shout, not only the regulation "hurrah for five and forty more," but for beating the best record. The bells were rung, the whistle blown, and throats rasped hoarse by shouting. Up to this time, the catch of twenty-seven whales by Capt. L. C. Owen, in 1881, was "high hook."

The morning of October 5th we were becalmed under East Cape, Siberia. Three other vessels were in sight on the American shore in the same predicament. Steam gave us an advantage, and before noon we were below the Straits and actually out of the Arctic Ocean.

On the morning of July 10th, when I went on deck, I found myself in the Arctic Ocean. I had looked into the ocean before, but this was my first actual being within its waters. I knew that old whalemen—men who had braved every sort of danger—the storm, reef, hurricane—dreaded no place more than this. I knew that its gales were terrific, its fogs dangerous, and its ice treacherous. I knew also that victims were called for unceremoniously, and that shipwreck, with possible loss of life, was a foregone conclusion every year. There were over twelve hundred men in the fleet, yet not one of us could feel that he was beyond the call of wreck. Day after day had come and gone. We had followed the whales into their haunts, though beset on all sides with the dangerous ice. The wily northeast current had grasped two or three vessels and carried them to the verge of destruction, then delivered them up to safety. A heavy fog had dropped down on the fleet, and kept everybody in suspense for over a week. Then came the spreading out. Vessels had scattered all the way along the edge of the pack, even off into the northwest beyond Herald Island. One whale after another had been picked up, until we reached our full capacity. Saying good-bye to all things, we emerged from the Arctic amazed at its gentleness. The gauntlet had been beset with snares, yet everybody ran it successfully. The furies seemed to have been suddenly tamed. Two or three bad winds had been experienced, but they were mild for Arctic blows.

It is a weight lifted from every man's heart to feel that he is below the Straits homeward bound.

There had been nothing to lead me to further fear the Arctic. I had not seen any particularly brilliant aurora borealis; there had not been any snow or other reminder such as one would expect at the approach of winter. East Cape and the Diomedes were barely tinged with white, and Indian Point, which we reached the next morning, gave no more evidences of winter than it did when I saw it in June. We had had three narrow escapes from wreck, but we might have had as serious experiences in any other sea.

It is a custom among many of the vessels that ship natives, to save the flukes of one whale for each. In this way food enough to last well into the winter is obtained. The *Orca* had three natives, but they got, besides their flukes, considerable blubber that had been left over. When we dropped anchor under Indian Point the sea was too rough for more than the most courageous of the men to come out in whale-boats. But they were overjoyed at the sight of the blubber, and worked vigorously until the last particle was in their boats. The sight was one never to be forgotten. Some pitched it up out of the blubber room, others dropped it over into the boats, and the rest stowed it away to the best advantage. Those on deck rather had the best of it, for they could cut off an occasional piece, or suck the oil off their fingers to take the edge off their appetites. The men in the blubber room got besmeared from head to foot with drippings, while those in the boat had an occasional piece of blubber dropped on them by way of variety. In spite of these side plays, the work went merrily on until it was finished.

The one great question that irritates the Eskimo mind is, how to get enough to eat. The dependence of these people upon the whalemen is well shown by the remark of one of the men to me: "I b'lieve no whale-ship, Masinker man all die."

There was a very noticeable change in the appearance of these people since I last saw them. They had discarded their old dirty clothes of summer, and put on new winter suits, which were neat and clean; most of them wore water-proofs, as the day was damp. The whole settlement turned out and lined the beach, awaiting revelations. That the sight of the blubber-tickled the Masinker appetite was evident from the sort of war-cry that was raised. Then all sat down on the sand and feasted, and they were still eating when we sailed, two hours afterward.

The lower part of Behring Sea, through which we were to pass, particularly off St. Matthew's and St. Paul's Islands, is usually a very stormy place in the fall of the year, so the ship was made ready for the worst; but it did not come, and there was nothing to interfere with the work necessary to be done. The "gums" had to be scraped off the whalebone; then the ship had to undergo a thorough scrubbing outside and in. After this, followed the washing and drying of the whalebone. It was soaked for forty-eight hours in salt water, then thoroughly scrubbed with hot salt water, rinsed, dried, and packed away.

A shorter course than through the "seventy-two" passage was through Ounimak Pass. As we approached the pass, the islands were nearly concealed by fog, but as we drew abreast of the Island of Ounimak, the fog lifted and the volcano came out in bold relief against a dark blue sky. Being 5,525 feet high, it was a grand sight, and as Captain Bauldry said he had never seen it before, though he had passed it probably twenty times, we both accepted the event as a very pretty compliment and greeting.

In going through the Straits, into the Pacific, I saw a most marvelous effect. The night was intensely dark, and we were going under full head of steam between high, overshadowing shores. The water was saturated with phosphorescence, and as the propellor churned up the sea, it made a luminous wake, extending astern of us, which extended far into the darkened distance. The effect was startling and wierd.

Some work was necessary on the ship before entering port. The crow's nest was taken down and stowed away for next year, the masts were scraped down and varnished, the engine and boilers cleaned and inspected, and, at the last moment, the sails all unbent and stowed away. And just before entering port, we shed our skin clothing and put on our "shore clothes."

On the morning of October 25th we steamed into San Francisco harbor, being the first whaler

A WHALESHIP IN THE ICE TRYING OUT OIL.   Page 112.

to arrive. I had been gone two hundred and thirty-six days, of which eighty-seven were spent within the Arctic Ocean. During the whole time I had experienced only the best of everything. The oldest whalemen in the Arctic could not remember such a remarkable year. Everything seemed to be exceptional, and I experienced and saw more in this one year than I could see in three average years. I had seen nothing of the hardships of Arctic whaling, yet enough to convince me that no men deserve what money they earn more than do these. Even the severe gales passed me by. Part of the fleet experienced one of the most terrific gales for years on October 2d, but I was up at the edge of the pack enjoying most perfect weather. We were quietly whaling, while ships considerably less than one hundred miles distant were in the fiercest of the gale.

Thirty-two vessels were in the fleet this year, fourteen of them owned in New Bedford, the other eighteen in San Francisco, and all returned. It was one of the very few years in the history of Arctic whaling when every vessel that sailed returned to port.

CHAPTER VI.

THE NAKOORUKS.

Little is known of the Nakooruks, as no systematic study of their life and customs has ever been undertaken. Several observing men, however, have lived among them for periods varying from one to three years, and from their observations, together with my own, I gather the following:

The Eskimo who inhabit Northern Alaska call themselves Innuit, singular Innuk, meaning the people. This would indicate that they have regarded themselves as the sole inhabitants of the earth world, or, perhaps, as the "chosen people." But this name is never applied in every-day use. It may give them a scientific classification under the general name Eskimo, but their common name, and the one by which they are known to whalemen and traders, is Nakooruk. This is their word for "good," and as they applied it to themselves when whalemen first invaded the Arctic, probably to indicate that they were good, or peaceable, it has got fastened to them as their name. Those that live inland are often called "deermen" to distinguish them from the "fishermen," or those who live along the coast. The former seldom meet white men, and consequently are diffident and unobtrusive, while many among the latter are learning the impudent importance of some of the traders and sailors with whom they come in contact. Some keen observers claim to see a difference between the deermen and the fishermen, and hold that the former show marked indications of American Indian blood, while there are not striking indications of its presence along the coast, except in instances where deermen have become fishermen.

The land of the Nakooruks begins in the vicinity of Port Clarence, and extends eastward as far, perhaps, as the Mackenzie River, though this is surmise, as nothing is known of the region beyond Point Barrow. The inland limits are vague, owing to a lack of knowledge of the country, and the nomadic habits of the people. Many families live on the road. They go and come wherever the best hunting is. Fishing is a more stable occupation, and some deermen about Kotzebue Sound have permanent abodes along the banks of the rivers that they inhabit during the run of fish. As far as I saw the country, there was not a sign of a tree from Cape Prince of Wales to Point Barrow. I am told, however, that the river banks back from Kotzebue Sound are wooded with a stunted growth. Above this, no trees are known to exist. Shrubs are found, particularly a sort of scrub willow that grows along the river banks, but this never exceeds ten feet in height, or one's arm in size. This willow spreads out over the ground, and wherever it touches it takes root.

In this desolate region there are, perhaps, two thousand five hundred people, at an approximate estimate. When at Cape Smyth, I saw a family that well illustrated their life. Three years before, it was living near Kotzebue Sound, then it packed up and went inland deer-hunting. It wandered about from one point to another, and this spring appeared where I saw it. What the next move would be, probably not one of the family could tell. The ruins of igaloos and settlements indicate that at some time the population must have been much larger. Without doubt, the presence of the whaling fleet has done much toward decimating their numbers.

The average native is constitutionally lazy, and if he can beg a meal to-day he forgets that he should be at work laying up food for the cold, long winter soon to come. Before the government had a revenue cutter in these waters, large quantities of vile whisky were sold by unprincipled traders, and the natives consumed so much time in drinking it that the hunting season was allowed to pass, and starvation was thus brought on. But other agencies have also aided in this decimation. The introduction of fire-arms has driven most of the deer far inland, many natives following. Whalemen have practically driven the walruses from the shore, and greatly reduced the numbers of hair-seals and whales. Thus all the supplies of food have been curtailed. In addition, disease has been introduced by the white men. All these causes, together with the great mortality among children, much of it natural, but, in some instances, intentional, have caused several years of famine and death.

In summer, when the ships are about, or there is hunting, the winter quarters are deserted, and with a few household utensils, a toopick, and the trade, the families move about from point to point as desire directs. The half-dozen points about which the ships congregate at times present a very lively appearance. But when they sail, the toopicks are packed up and pitched elsewhere. When the cold weather comes on, and the creeks begin to freeze over, the families return to their winter homes.

One of the largest settlements is at the very gateway to the Arctic Ocean, on the sand-spit at the end of Cape Prince of Wales. The natives here have always been more treacherous and warlike than the others until within a few years, and they are still feared and mistrusted by their neighbors. They formerly waged war upon everybody within reach, and were sullen and menacing to the whalemen. This was especially true until they met a sudden check at the hands of Capt. George Gilley. How this happened is best given in Mr. Gilley's own words.

CAPTAIN GILLEY AND THE CAPE PRINCE OF WALES NATIVES.

"I came up in 1878 in the brig *William H. Allen*, on a whaling and trading voyage. I reached East Cape early in July. I then started to cross the Straits, but a thick fog came on. The current carried us into shoal water, so we dropped anchor. Soon a canoe load of Prince of Wales natives came along-side, and the chief waved a skin on a pole, indicating a desire to trade. When he got on board he wanted ammunition. I got some, and, after he had shot at cakes of ice for awhile, he asked me to give him five cartridges for his repeating rifle. This I refused to do, though I offered to trade. It was quite noticeable that he and some of his followers were under the influence of liquor.

"The chief was about six feet five inches tall, by far the most powerful native we had ever seen. I knew that he was a murderous villain, and that his followers would do just what he told them to. This, in addition to the indications of liquor, put me on my guard. Meantime, two other canoe-loads came aboard, and with them was the chief that stood next in authority. All began to ask for rum, but I told them that I had none. They said that they knew I had, for all ships with two masts had it.

"One fellow, apparently accidentally, fell overboard, and though a canoe was towing astern, the chief wanted me to lower a boat and rescue him. I said no. He then asked me to go into the cabin. Again I said no. At this, he grasped me by the throat, but when I drew a revolver, he let go, and stepping off, smiled as though it was a joke. Things indicated that there was to be trouble, so I stationed two men near me, each armed with a hand-spike. There was not a breath of air stirring, yet I ordered the anchor hove up. When the crew attempted to execute the order, the natives stopped them. Then the chief sent his wife with the other women and old men into the canoe. This meant a fuss. He then seized me again by the throat, and I told one of the men to tap him on the head with a hand-spike. The tap killed him.

"The other natives were on the main deck, and suddenly each drew a single-barreled muzzle-loading pistol and began to shoot and chase

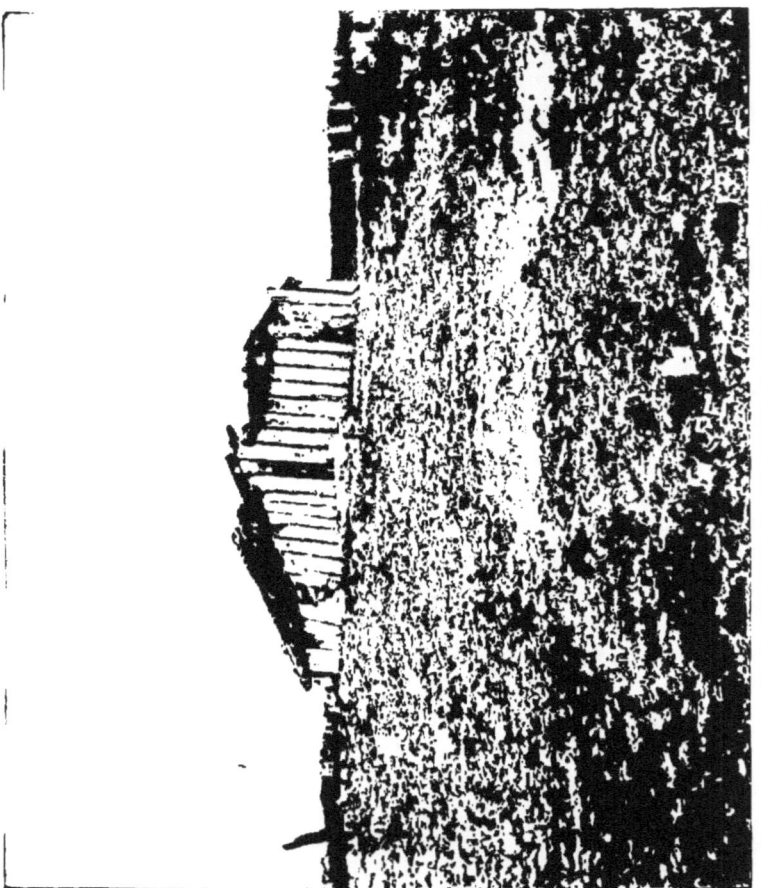

THE DANCE HALL AT POINT BARROW.—Page 115.

the crew about. Prompt action was necessary. I knocked over the other chief with my revolver and called for my rifle. After the natives had emptied their pistols they resorted to big knives and stabbed one sailor in the back. I stood ready, and whenever I saw a native raise his knife I shot him. They had not expected this, and, balked in their attempt to take the vessel, they endeavored to escape. But their canoes had got adrift. A light breeze sprang up, and heaving anchor, we got under way. Their one desire seemed to be to conceal themselves, and all crawled under the t'gallant forecastle. I intended to take the survivors prisoners, carry them to the Siberian shore and land them, for they had been punished enough, but the instant I laid down my rifle, they tried to use their knives on me. Seeing no other alternative, I posted men above them, and when a native showed his head, he was clubbed and thrown overboard. Toward the last we hauled them out with gaff hooks. The three canoes had contained about twenty warriors, but not one of them had escaped. Afterward I learned that these same men had looted Captain Jacobson's schooner a week before, and tried to take Captain Raven's brig. They had also endeavored to take possession of two other ships.

"I had two Siberian natives in my crew, and when we got back to East Cape they spread the news of the affair, and by the next season the affair was known to all natives on both shores. No attempt to take a vessel has been made since. I had one man killed. Two others were cut, but not seriously so."

In Kotzebue Sound is another settlement. It is on the end of the sand-spit at the entrance to Hotham Inlet, and consists of perhaps a dozen igaloos. In summer, however, it is a great meeting place for the natives of all the country about, even as far as Point Hope, the Diomedes, and Port Clarence. Here they exchange trade, gossip, etc., and do more or less fishing.

Point Hope is the next settlement, though there are a few scattered igaloos between. The sand-spit, on the end of which it is situated, juts boldly out into the Arctic Ocean. There are twenty-five or thirty inhabited igaloos and four or five that are in ruins or deserted.

Three miles above Cape Lisburne is a collection of half a dozen, or so, igaloos, and each will average five or six families. Usually an igaloo is not much over twelve feet square, but these are about twenty.

Eight igaloos, some of them very small, are situated fifteen miles below Point Lay, while at the Point itself are four igaloos. The natives here spend a greater part of their time inland, or elsewhere, hunting, and their habitations are occupied only a short time during the year.

Half way to Icy Cape is a settlement of a dozen igaloos on the inside of the lagoon. The Cape is a summer trading station, but there is not an igaloo nearer than this settlement below, or one fifteen miles above, where there is a collection of a dozen or fifteen. These are either deserted or very little used.

Twenty-five miles below Wainwright Inlet are fifteen to eighteen igaloos, and on the shores of the inlet, a mile and a half from its mouth, are a dozen or so.

The twenty or more igaloos at Point Belcher are all occupied, but at Point Franklin, just above, are two deserted settlements of a dozen or fifteen huts each; one is about six miles from the Point, the other ten miles farther north. These habitations are all tumbled in. The natives do not know how long these settlements have been deserted, their conception of time is too vague, but Captain Owen thinks two huts were occupied in 1877, for he remembers going ashore to trade. Probably the decay of these settlements dates from the great wreck season. Not only were many natives poisoned by drinking the contents of the medicine chests at that time, but many more moved away out of superstitious fear. The population here has been reduced at least one-half in twenty years.

The next settlement is at Cape Smyth, where there are perhaps thirty igaloos, though many are not inhabitable, and at Point Barrow are still fewer; but in the former are thirty-two families, while in the latter are thirty-six, and a considerably larger population. Four huts at the Point are occupied by one family each, leaving close quarters for the remaining twenty-eight families, particularly as the huts there are smaller than those at the Cape. Back of Point Barrow is a deserted settlement of fifteen or more igaloos. Most of the inhabitants there are believed to have died off, and it is probable that the remnant moved to the Point. It is only recently that this abandonment took place, for when whalemen first visited Point Barrow there were four hundred or more natives there. Between the Cape and the Point is another summer trading place, called the "Shooting Station," from the many ducks that fly there. This summer it was very flourishing, having at least seventy toopicks at one time. Families came a hundred miles or more, and among them were several who had never seen white men before.

About one hundred and twenty-five miles east of Point Barrow is another of these trading places, and two-thirds of the way to the Mackenzie River is Barter Island. How large or important a place this is can only be guessed at, for it has not been visited by white men since the days of Sir John Franklin. There are no permanent settlements known east of Point Barrow until the Mackenzie River is reached.

Each Eskimo householder is an independent sovereign, and free to go as he pleases. There is no law, no chief, no tribunal, or other power to hold or command him; but he instinctively observes the rule of doing as he would be done by. There is no ownership in land, hence each household is a commune in itself. Jealousy of each other is the only tie that keeps the settlements intact and equal. Orphan children are always adopted into other families, and treated as natural offspring. As a general rule, everything is peace and harmony, not only between the settlements, but between the households. Such civilized evils as tobacco or whisky lead to quarrels, and, at rare intervals, a jealous or quarrelsome woman is believed to need toning down with a few blows. Murder leads to a feud between the families of the principals, and may be handed down from father to son until the immediate families are both all murdered off for the sake of revenge.

Most naturally, every settlement has its leading spirit, and it is always he of the largest property. He holds his position because he has in his employ, and under his protection, a larger number of men than any other person. But should he have the misfortune to lose his property through famine, poor trade, or exces-

THE NAKOORUKS. 151

sive doctor's bills, he forfeits his position. Keewuck is the best trader at Point Belcher; Mung-gi and Unggeroo are prominent whalemen at Cape Smyth. Unalena takes the lead at Point Barrow, though Ap-i-yau is an expert whaleman. Point Hope also has its expert tradesman, trader, and whalemen. For the sake of a name whalemen call these men "chiefs."

The habitation of the Nakooruk differs from that of the other Eskimo. Instead of being a skin or a snow hut, it is a hole dug in the ground and roofed over. It is called an igaloo. It is usually about seven or eight feet deep, and from ten to fifteen feet square. Logs of driftwood form the frame-work to keep the sides from caving in, and logs are also laid down to form the floor. The roof is either of wood or the jaw-bones of the whale, over which is stretched a covering of hide, protected by a thick covering of sods. The "eaves" are just above the ground, and the center is a little higher still. A window of a yard or so square is cut out in the middle of the roof, and strips from the intestines of animals are sewed together as a substitute for glass. A small wooden pipe serves to carry off some of the smoke and foul air. When more ventilation becomes necessary, the women use fans of geese wings, or other material, and force fresh air from the outside entrance through the room.

Beginning fifteen or twenty feet off, a trench is dug toward the hut, reaching the depth of a yard below the level of the floor. This is roofed over, except at the outer end, which serves as the entrance. About a yard from the wall within the hut, is an oval hole in the floor about three feet long, so that, to enter the hut, one goes through this trench, then stoops down and crawls up through this hole. At the outside of this entrance is a cover to keep out the snow and wind. Then there is a shifting board to regulate the draft. An igaloo usually contains two families, sometimes three, but seldom only one. The families are not necessarily related, but congenial to each other, so that they travel and hunt together. An approximate average to an igaloo would be ten persons. The owner of the abode often has sleeping accommodations for himself and wife in the entrance-way, but his children sleep inside with the other occupants.

THE MOST NORTHERN HABITATION OF NORTH AMERICA.—Page 118.

Extending across the opposite side of the room from the entrance hole, is a platform raised a yard from the floor. The top of this is used as a sort of sitting-room, and for extra sleeping accommodations. The occupants of the hut sleep underneath it on the floor. On the outside comes the man, then comes his wife, beyond are the children, ranged according to size, the youngest being next the wife. It is seldom that a family numbers over five children. Deer-skin blankets serve as bedding, and after stowing themselves away between these — the hair sides being together — the natives remove all the clothing worn during the day.

Every igaloo has its "stove" or "lamp," sometimes two or more, which stands in the corner or at one side of the room. Lamps were formerly made of stone, but wood is much used now. They are crescent-shaped on top and perhaps three feet from point to point. They are scooped out on top an inch and a half or so, to hold the oil; fuel-moss is placed around the edge, the roots running down into the oil, thus serving as a wick. When this moss is lighted, it slowly tries the oil out of a piece of blubber that hangs the proper distance above, thus replenishing the oil that is burned. The quantity of fire is graded by the amount of moss used.

Generally, the richer the man, the better his igaloo. He may not only have a larger one than the average, but a better entrance-way, with perhaps a store-room or kitchen opening into it.

When returning to his winter hut after the summer season, the native goes about cutting a small chip off every piece of timber and board that can be reached easily. The significance of this is probably to break whatever spell the devil may have cast over the abode during the absence of its occupants. When deserted in the spring, the window is broken in, the entrance-way blocked up, and rubbish thrown in, to give it the appearance of having been abandoned, probably to throw the devil off the scent.

Back from the sea-coast the natives do not build igaloos. When intending to remain in one place any length of time in winter, they usually build a snow hut. At all other times a portable deer-skin tent serves for protection and deer-skin blankets, instead of bags, for bedding.

During the summer the Nakooruk household lives in a toopick, or tent, made of sail-cloth, though in exceptional cases, of skins. It is pitched near the winter abode, except when off hunting or on other expeditions. In some instances I have seen the canoe turned up and used temporarily to live under.

It is a severe ordeal for native babies to get into the world and survive the first few months, but when they once get a grip on life their lot is a comparatively happy one. A woman in childbirth is put off apart from everybody else in a little shanty, and left for fate to decide whether she shall be safely delivered, or, not only her own, but the child's life be sacrificed. This is the ordeal, whether it be winter or summer. Old women acts as nurses and see that food is placed within reach of the patient. There their attentions usually cease. When the babe begins to show signs of life the old women take it in hand, roll it in the mud, or snow, according to whether it be winter or summer, then leave it there all naked for an hour or two to kick about and provide amusement for the dogs. This is undoubtedly intended for an acclimating process. They then give vent to howling and chanting to drive away evil spirits that may be born with it, or that threaten it. Even when the child survives this ordeal, it is not fully initiated into all the rites and ceremonies of Nakooruk existence, for it may next be sewed up in a skin bag of the blouse and trowsers pattern, with only its head sticking out. I saw one child two months old dressed only in a hood and much abbreviated shirt, both of squirrel-skin. At times it would be stowed snugly away in its mother's gown, but again, she would lay it in her lap.

There is no cradle for the baby to be rocked in, nor rattle to attract its attention. When the cry comes, the mother, or some other woman, will take the child on her back, carry it out into the breeze, and let it face that for a while (for the Nakooruk child looks over its mother's shoulder, instead of being carried back to back as is the case with the American Indians). If the north wind does not happen to blow a chilly gale, so as to freeze the child's cry, a few pokes in the back induce gentle slumbers.

As soon as the child is able to sit up, its schooling begins. The mother sits on the floor, with her feet out before her to brace the baby against them, then teaches it to swing its arms in all directions, particularly over its head. Then follow lessons in the native chanting, dancing, etc. Nursing is kept up for several years. To see a child five or six years old nursing is a common occurrence. In the case of favorite children, they are nursed until they are perhaps ten years old.

When a girl is ten or twelve years old a narrow blue line is tattooed from the lip down the face of her chin, and as she grows older the line is broadened, and ultimately, in most cases, a narrow line is added each side of the broad one. At about the same age the lips of the boys are pierced. A small ivory button, or labret, is worn just below each corner of his mouth, and the hole is gradually enlarged, so that by the time he is grown up it is plenty large enough to put the end of his little finger through.

There is but one system of doctoring sick children. The medicine man puts on a most horrible black mask, then goes into the presence of the child and chants and howls in his most unearthly tones. This over, he goes outside and walks around and around the hut, still chanting and beating the drum to drive off the evil spirits. The drums that I heard sounded about as musical as the so-called "devil's fiddle" (a tin can with a resined string in the bottom of it).

In spite of all these drawbacks, children come into the world fast, many women having a child every summer. Lung troubles are very prevalent, being caused by the sudden changes in going from the hot igaloo into the intense cold. But probably the severest part of the Nakooruk's ordeal in getting himself into the proper attitude to exist, is to accustom his stomach to meat that is putrid, frozen, raw, boiling hot, or in some other condition, as he eats not only a sufficiency, but probably to excess at all times. The long period of nursing is undoubtedly necessary to accustom the child to a steady meat diet.

Children are very much doted on, never refused anything, never whipped, never reprimanded. Consequently, they have no cause for fear, or deception, and grow up without knowing how to steal or lie. There are instances in which traders have left their sleds unguarded for days in a settlement, and not missed anything, though there was a large stock of articles which natives covet most. Where there is much intercourse with the white men, some of the natives do steal, but they get the credit sometimes of stealing, when the crime is committed by some sailor, and the article traded to the native.

Before a mother eats, she will first offer the food to her child, perhaps touching its lips with it. If the child is out of doors, the mother will often leave the hut, and go through this ceremony, before partaking of food. Old women consider it a duty to criticise each child very carefully, and compare its points with those of other children.

Life seems solely for personal gratification. This is shown in the looseness of what might be called the marriage relation. A man may live with most of the marriageable women of the settlement before taking one to wife, and even then, it may not be for good, as she may conclude after awhile to live with another man. There appears to be very little appreciation of virtue or morality in either sex. If a man is going off on a journey, and his wife is not able to accompany him, he borrows from his neighbor, and returns her when the journey is ended. Should a child result from this borrowing, there is no scandal, but a relationship exists thenceforth between the two families as though they had a common ancestor. A man or a woman with children is more marriageable than one who is childless, for every child means so much help to keep the spark of life aglow. No questions are asked as to the parentage of children. Men and women both enter into so many matrimonial ventures that such inquiry would be useless. There may be children in the family that are not in any way related to their supposed parents.

The Nakooruk probably does not exist who has not been married. In exceptional cases, a man may have two or three wives, not because he has property, and can afford to support them—for the women frequently support the men—but because he can control them and keep them from fighting. Many men do not take a second wife because one proves too much to subdue. Far up the coast, polygamy

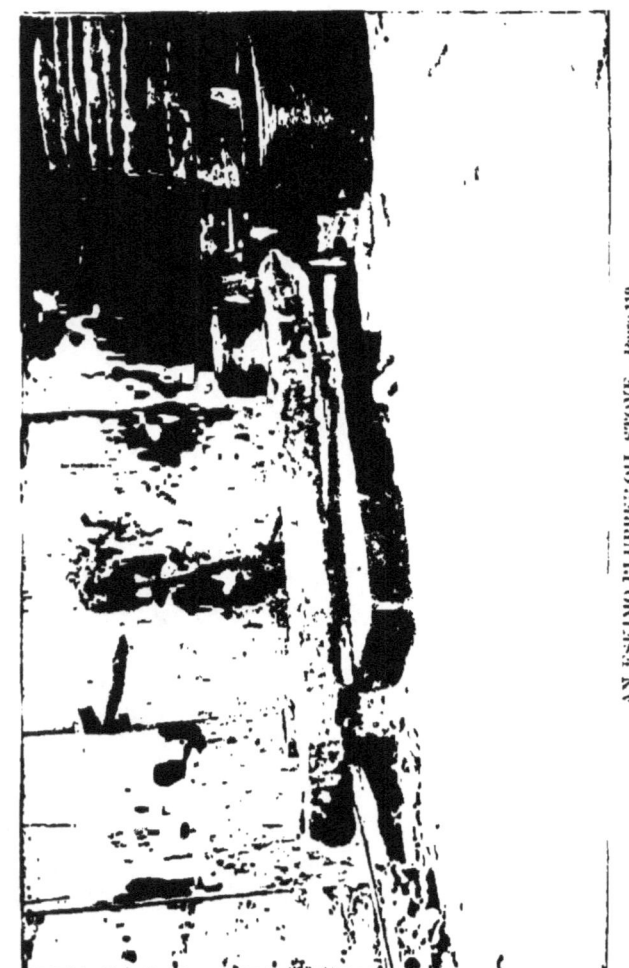

AN ESKIMO BLUBBER-OIL STOVE.—Page 119.

is but little practiced. Only one man at Point Barrow has two wives, while at Cape Smyth all the men are monogamists. The chief at Point Hope, At-tung-aw-rah, has five wives, and is probably the most married man on the coast. In cases of polygamy, the children belong equally to all the wives, and should two wives have children about the same time, they nurse either one, whether it be their own or not. The great terror in many families is the mother-in-law. She may drive a man into abandoning his wife, or the wife may be driven off by the husband's mother. One medicine man told me that the only patient he had cured in a long time was his mother-in-law, but the cure was not lasting, and he was so astonished at his own skill, that he declined his services the next time she required them, consequently she died. "Yes, she die. Me glad. Me no care," said he.

When a man wants a wife, he goes to the parents of the girl he wishes to marry, and if they are agreeable to the match, she has to go whether she wants to or not. They live together possibly the rest of their lives, but more probably he will get tired of her, and desert her so as to take another woman that he thinks he likes better. Perhaps, however, the wife may leave him. If a girl has no parents, she contracts whatever matrimonial alliances she likes.

All is not a sober struggle for existence, as games are prevalent, and much indulged in. Foot-ball is played with a bag stuffed with hair. "Tag" is the same game the world over. Children are fond of "teetering," standing upon the end of the plank instead of sitting down. Another amusement, which requires skill, is tossing up in a blanket. A walrus-hide is used, and the contest of skill is to see who can stand on his feet and be tossed into the air the highest. Small children have miniature sleds which they load with mice-skins, and all sorts of trinkets, so as to play trader. Boys practice archery. Of course, they slide down hill, but the sled is the seat of a stout pair of deer-skin trousers. Athletics are also much indulged in. One difficult feat is to walk on the hands, the legs being outside of the arms, and held straight out in front, parallel with the ground. Lifting matches are frequent, but very few natives are as strong as the average white man. Hurling the spear is also practiced, and small darts guided by goose feathers are thrown with great accuracy, often hitting a mark at thirty feet. The faculty to throw a stone, either with a sling or by hand, is innate in every boy. In fact, the festive small boy is the same the world over.

Girls play with dolls carved out of ivory, which they dress up after their own fashion, in clothing of ermine, mice, or other skins. One of their games is to kick a ball of ice or snow about the size of a base-ball, the object being to keep it in the air all the time without touching it with their hands. They also toss pebbles very skilfully, some being able to keep six or seven in the air at a time, with one hand. They frequently wear bracelets of sinew, on which are strung bits of iron, brass, or anything that will jingle. Stones are tossed in the air, the hands crossing each other between the tosses, jingling the bracelets, keeping time and accompanying the play with a sort of chant.

Many young girls do nice sewing. At Port Clarence they make bags of squirrel, seal, ermine and other skins to trade with the ships. It falls to the girls to care for the young orphan pups, and as a substitute for nursing, they will chew up seal or other meat, then pucker their lips, and let the dog suck them to get the meat.

Even the women have a game to resort to occasionally to vary the monotony of drudgery. They lock elbows, or fingers, then place their feet against each other's shoulders and pull to test their strength.

Old and young, male and female, are passionately fond of cards, and are inveterate players. Their chief game is a corruption of "Russian seven-up." They also play an imitation of poker. No game is played without stakes, which usually consist of a bead, match, chew of tobacco, or the like. If sides are played and a partner is lacking, a baby is pressed into service, the partner doing the playing for the child.

Time is reckoned by winters, moons and sleeps. In winter, habits are regular, hence account of time is easily kept; but in summer, when wandering about, and sleeping whenever and wherever the inclination wills, it is difficult to keep the sleeps. A record is kept on the rafters to the roofs in the huts, which shows the age of the structure, a peg being driven in to represent each winter, or possibly a notch cut.

Just what the Nakooruks worship is very difficult to discover, for they are very jealous and superstitious about such matters. Good and bad spirits are believed in, though very little regard, apparently, seems to be paid to the former. Sickness is caused by evil spirits getting possession of a person. These evil spirits, or the devil—for there seems to be no difference between them—may infect anything. If a man goes hunting and makes poor shots, the devil is believed to have cast his spell over the rifle, and it becomes necessary to resort to chanting and its accompaniments to restore the rifle to good shooting condition. The devil is never visible, but is heard in every suspicious noise or place, hence he is greatly feared. He is called Toonook, which means something like "spirit of death." He is believed to be the spirit of some being or animal that formerly lived. The good spirit is called Kelligabuk, which means mastodon. As this animal is venerated as a sort of "god of the hunting grounds," it is suggested that the lip ornaments are worn as an imitation of its tusks. A future existence is believed in, in which every one will be happy, successful in the hunt, and have plenty to eat, which includes a goodly supply of tobacco and, with many, not too short a supply of liquor. Turquois beads are much worn as a guard against the evil spirits. Where the beads came from the natives themselves do not know, neither do they know where the charm comes in, but the custom has come down from one generation to another and the bead continues to serve the same purpose. Being scarce, these beads are the best of trade. The existence of witches and ghosts is thoroughly believed in, and their presence is continually guarded against, especially when a death occurs. On such occasions windows and doors are all religiously closed, to shut out these intruders and perhaps to keep out that greater terror, the devil.

Just before the ice breaks up in the spring, or before the deer begin to run, or before any such annual event which plays an important part in their existence, the Eskimo beat drums, and go through incantations, in order to bring about the event, and the ceremony gets the credit for what nature's yearly routine invariably brings to pass.

The extent to which their superstition goes

is well illustrated by a horrible ceremony witnessed by a white man at Point Hope in May, 1885. Several crews of natives had been off whaling, and when they returned it was learned that a woman had died during their absence. This led them to fear that they would not get another whale until the dead woman's heart was cut out, rolled up in a seal-skin and thrown into the sea. Three old women were appointed to the task of performing this ceremony. They blackened their faces about their eyes, made a black mark across their foreheads and one down each cheek, probably to conceal their identity, then went to work. The body was laid out, and, with stone knives, two gashes were cut, one across the pit of the stomach, and the other at right angles, crossing it at the center. The four corners were then pinned back with sticks, and with a forked stick the heart was reached, cut out, and carefully rolled up in seal-skin. Great care was taken not to allow the fingers to touch the heart or the body. With the heart thus secured, they marched solemnly in single file over the ice and out to the water, chanting all the while. Then they threw the heart into the sea.

As the whole operation had been satisfactorily performed, the men manned their canoes the next day, and, unfortunately, returned at night with a whale, thus strengthening their belief in the efficacy of the ceremony.

The men are stoics when in pain or trouble, never giving up to their feelings, whatever may befall them, or whatever predicament they may be in. The same spirit is shown in keeping an agreement. When a native gives his word he keeps it if it is in his power to do so. The women, on the other hand, give up at the least discouragement, and give vent to most pitiful howls and groans, and perhaps have hysterics.

Medicine men often hand their vocation down to their sons, all usually practicing it. When called in case of sickness, the medicine man sets himself apart from the patient to chant, howl, and otherwise get himself into the proper state of mind, also to induce the friends of the sick to lay before him a plentiful supply of cloth, rifles, furs, and other valuables. His mood seems to be about right when the pay is sufficient. He then enters the presence of the patient, chants, howls, beats a hideous sounding drum, and in other ways endeavors to drive

WASHING WHALEBONE.—Page 135.

away the evil spirit, or spirits that have brought on the illness.

In the midst of the ceremony he may take a short rest, partly to get breath, but more particularly to give the friends a chance to increase the fee. Should the patient die, the whole fee must be returned, but if the patient recovers, the medicine man takes everything that was placed before him. The usual fee ranges from $10 to $20 in trade. I learned of one instance where the fee was nearly $1,000 worth of trade. A rich family may be reduced to the verge of starvation in a very short time by sickness. Naturally medicine men are the most prosperous in the settlement. Shrewd young men see "millions in it" and consequently go into it. But the profession is getting crowded. A prosperous medicine man refuses to take a case unless recovery is practically assured, and an aged or infirm person may expect no favors at his hands. But frequently a young practitioner will take a case that has been refused by some eminent competitor, and bring about recovery. His reputation is then made.

The lot of the aged is hard, and frequently

natural death is anticipated. If an old hunter is beyond his usefulness, he may ask a medicine man, or perhaps some personal friend, to kill him. Or, when food is scarce, old people are turned out to starve, whether they are anxious to die or not. If turning these out does not suffice, the superfluous women are also turned out. Thus the winter of 1885-6 was an unusually severe one at Point Hope, owing to a shorter supply of food than usual. A dreadful famine ensued, and resulted in not only aged persons being cast out, but also many women, including plural wives, who did not stand in high favor, and their babes, being turned out to die. There has since been a scarcity of women there. During this famine many dogs were eaten, and in some instances the walrus-hide coverings to canoes were cut up and made into soup. Old women are usually gossips of the worst type. The weight of years seems also to bring to them unfortunate habits, one particularly noticeable habit being that of picking lice out of the heads of children, eating the large ones, and putting the others back to fatten.

The dead are cared for according to the

respect in which they were held. The body of a favorite child might be protected from the ravages of the dogs all winter, then buried when the ground would admit.. But if the child were not a favorite, the body would be dragged a short distance from the settlement and left to the mercies of the dogs. This is true of all ages, as well as children. Effort is made to prevent death occurring in a hut, but if it does occur, the body is removed through a hole cut in the side of the hut, which is closed up after the body is removed. This is probably done that the spirit may not find its way back. In instances of this kind the hut is frequently deserted. The personal property of the dead, particularly hunting-gear, tobacco, and trade, is laid away with the body, but broken or ruined beyond further use. Whatever remains goes to the relatives. Every member of the family mourns for four days, after a death in their midst, and no work is done except what is absolutely necessary. Should the family be making a journey, this custom will be observed as closely as the circumstances will allow. No member of an afflicted family will go into the hut of another family until a change in the moon, for fear of communicating death. Black stones, or other substances, may be put on the eyes of the dead, perhaps that the light may not be seen, or that the dead spirit may be blinded so far as earthly affairs are concerned.

All food is obtained by hunting, and along the shore deer are shot in considerable numbers. When winter is ushered in by an easterly wind, the deer hurry inland to the mountains and ravines, so that but few are killed. At other times they wander along the shore, and many are killed and stowed away for winter use. In summer they migrate north, but as the cold weather returns they return south. Venison and fish form much of the diet on the coast. In the spring of 1887, eleven whales were caught at Point Barrow, so this much additional food was added to the store for the following winter. All meat is dressed and stowed down in caches, nearly every household having a cache. A cache has a small entrance at the top, but widens out to a considerable space at the bottom, and is ten feet, or so, deep. When no whales are caught at Point Barrow the natives are hard up for trade, for they lack ammunition and nearly everything else. One native never gives to another without expecting a present in return, even it be only a small piece of blubber. If the present is not forthcoming, particularly if a white man be concerned, the receiver of the gift is informed of the fact and told what will be acceptable in return. If too much delay takes place, the return of the present may be asked for, unless, unfortunately, it be food which may have been already digested.

A primitive method of catching deer is to build a large pen, or corral, of brush, drive a herd into it, then kill as many as possible, while they are attempting to escape. When a man is hunting alone, he frequently fastens a slip-noose of seal-skin line over a well-trodden deer path. The deer gets his antlers entangled in it and is thus captured and killed. If a native sees a deer alone, he crawls up on all fours until he gets within rifle range, if he can get there.

Another food supply is the seal; in fact, this is frequently the chief source of food in midwinter. There are three methods of catching seals besides shooting. Sometimes a pole, perhaps thirty feet long, that has a sharp ivory tip, is used. With this in hand, the native watches a breathing-hole frequented by seals, and the instant one shows its head, it is transfixed. Sometimes the native turns seal himself. With spear, or rifle in hand, he crawls toward a seal that lies sleeping on the ice. When it mistrusts his presence, he scratches on the ice with a hook (made of wood in the shape of a turkey's foot, and tipped with bear claws) in imitation of the scratching of the seal's flipper. Thinking it to be another seal, the creature goes to sleep again. And so the native wiggles his way along, occasionally flapping his foot on the ice in imitation of the seal's flippers, until it is too late for the seal to discover the deception. But there is another method more ingenious and original than either of these. A coarse meshed net of seal-skin roping is stretched under a much frequented breathing-hole. Being about five feet wide, and extending about a yard or so beyond the hole at each end, the net makes it impossible for the seal to dive straight down. A seal always floats along close to the ice till it reaches a hole, then it rises and breathes. But instead of floating off as it comes, it always dives when through breathing, and here is where it makes the fatal mistake. By so doing, it gets entangled in the meshes of the net, and is drowned. In this manner ten seals are sometimes captured at one hole in as many hours. Always when bringing home a seal, the native puts a dish of water to its lips, lets a few drops of water fall on it, then throws the water toward, or into, the sea. The significance of this is not known. A few walruses are occasionally caught on the Alaskan shore, and they are usually shot, though sometimes they are harpooned and buoyed up with a poke. The Eskimo is as much afraid of a walrus as he is of a whale.

When off hunting, or otherwise journeying, and the native is cold, or wants to do cooking, he gathers drift-wood or other fuel, and after getting it ready to light, he builds a guard of ice around it, perhaps square in shape, but leaving one side open to get at the fire. This "stove" furnishes more heat than one would imagine.

The Eskimo usually begin their whaling about the middle of April. At the different settlements the methods of carrying it on vary.

At Point Hope, the poke method is used almost entirely. The whalemen watch along the edge of the ground or shore ice, and when a whale appears, a harpoon with three pokes attached is thrown into it. The line to which the pokes are tied is only five or ten fathoms long. Every time the whale appears, another harpoon, with its three pokes, is thrown into him, and so on until four or five harpoons have been thrown. These are sufficient to buoy up an average whale. Whenever the opportunity offers, a lance, either ivory or steel pointed, or a blubber-spade, or perhaps a pole with a sharp knife tied to the end, is prodded into the whale until it is worried to death. All the canoes now join in towing the carcass ashore, or if shore can not be reached, to some convenient spot on the ice, where it can be cut in. Every particle is saved, even to the entrails.

At Point Barrow, the method of whaling is somewhat different, owing to the introduction of bomb-lances. The whalemen go out on the edge of the floe, or ice, and scatter themselves in camps. Their canoes are held on chutes of ice, and a man is braced at the head of each all day long. When a whale happens near

A FULL SUIT OF HAIR SEAL-SKIN. Page 136.

enough, the canoe, man, and all, are darted at it. The harpoon which the man darts into the whale has three pokes attached to it, and when it is made fast, the pole, or handle, which is twenty-five feet, or so, long, to which it is attached, is drawn out. The instant the boat is darted, a man on the ice shoots a bomb-lance into the whale with a shoulder-gun. If this does not kill, the whale is worried to death by more bombs, more pokes, and more lancing. Sometimes whales are bombed when no harpoons are thrown. Such carcasses do not float usually. The harpoons formerly used by the natives had flint heads set into shanks of bone or ivory about seven inches long, but now steel is used, instead of flint, and in many instances the regulation steel harpoons of the whale-ships are used.

Without dogs the Eskimo would be nearly helpless, consequently much attention is given to their breeding. The more wolf blood, the better the dog, both for faithfulness and endurance. After long breeding the old stock loses its quality. The offspring is lazy, useless for work, in short, a common cur. To keep up the quality, occasionally a young wolf is caught and reared to breed from. Wolf blood is apparent in all the dogs, yet they are susceptible of much training. I have seen a whole team sleep in a canoe loaded with venison, perhaps some of the dogs using it for a pillow, yet not touch it. One young dog that I saw in this position once forgot himself and tasted the meat, but I doubt if he ever forgot himself again, or the brutal pounding that was meted out at that time. There seems to be much truth in the remark one whaleman made, that an Eskimo will feed his dogs with a kicking and clubbing and expect them to grow fat on it.

The dogs sometimes amuse themselves by hunting, usually in pairs, after ground-squirrel. One will take a ridge of land where the holes are, and the other drive the game out of the grass below. When the squirrel is disturbed, and runs for his hole, the first dog seizes it and holds it until the second dog comes up. They each get a good grip with their teeth, and pull. Something must give, and each dog is entitled to as much as he may succeed in getting. Should a dog meet with an accident, such as falling into the water, another dog will go to his assistance, catch him by the nape of the neck, and haul him out, if possible.

The Eskimo are too cunning for the sly fox. A simple trap is the slip-noose plan. After digging a hole in the snow, perhaps a foot and a half deep, bait is tied to the end of a string and put in the bottom. The other end of the string is a slip-noose concealed in the snow about the edge of the hole, and the middle of the string passes through another string tied to a heavy weight. When the fox puts his head into the hole and jerks at the bait, he tightens the noose about his own neck and thus hangs himself. Another fox-catcher is made by fastening a curved stick between two ropes twisted tight, and held by a bobbin, which holds the bait, and springs it. The fox nibbles the bait, and releases the stick, which the twist in the ropes drops on his head like a sledge-hammer. Foxes, and likewise a species of ravens, live, for the most part, on field-mice, of which there are three kinds. Grouse are caught in the same net that is used in spring for seining salmon.

Jack rabbits are driven into an inclosure made of nets, then killed. These rabbits weigh ten or twelve pounds in the winter. Their fur then is a beautiful soft white, but in the summer it is gray. When a native wants to shoot one of these, he walks round and round, getting nearer each time, until close enough for a sure shot. The rabbit follows the hunter with its eyes, but does not notice his gradual approach.

During the winter the Eskimo have one meal daily. It begins when they get up, and, with a few intermissions, ends when they go to bed; one course after another is brought on, with the breathing spells between. When there are two dishes, one is for the men and the other for the women, but when only one dish, the men eat what they want, and the women have the leavings. The flesh of the whale, walrus, and deer, also fish, is best relished when raw, or simply warmed to thaw the frost out when frozen. Bear and seal meat is cooked, if the appetite can be held in check long enough. A sort of "crane" is hung near the "stove" to hold the kettle. The only way of cooking meat is boiling. If birds are to be cooked, only the larger feathers are pulled out, pin feathers and down being of too little consequence to bother about. Occasionally birds are skinned when the skins are wanted to make clothing, or to use for other purposes. The viscera are not removed until after the cooking is done. Deer have a parasite living between the skin on the back and the flesh, a sort of maggot, which is about one inch long. It is as great a delicacy to the Eskimo, whether raw or cooked, as shrimp is to the more civilized epicure. A curious dish is made of snow, salmon berries, and deer fat, mixed together. It looks like strawberry ice-cream, but tastes as coon meat would, were it four times its natural strength. Meat can be kept a long time. When got in summer it is put into caches, or buried in some shaded nook, where it remains frozen solid. In winter meat is simply hung up on poles out of the reach of the dogs and other animals. Tea has come to be in great demand, and both old and young are great consumers of it. Nothing short of eight or nine cups is really satisfying. Molasses, or sugar, is used for sweetening whenever obtainable. The use of milk is not known.

There is much fishing done along the coast, and, as a rule, seines are used. In some places tom-cod are plentiful, while in the rivers are salmon trout, whitefish, and a sort of pike that sometimes grows to a length of two feet or so. salmon run in the spring. Other kinds of fish are occasionally caught, so it can be said that the rivers are comparatively well stocked. In winter, frost-fish are caught with a hook and line above Point Hope. Sinew, or strips of whalebone tied together, form the fish lines, and the hooks are crooked pieces of wire fixed in a stone, shell, or piece of ivory. Perhaps two or three red beads serve as bait. A small shell with red spots makes an excellent hook, when fitted with wire, but as it comes from British Columbia and vicinity, through barter from one tribe to another, it is very expensive. What might be called spoon-hooks are used to troll for salmon.

Settlements exchange gossip through hunters and travelers, and news is much sought after. By this method, settlements know what is going on around them. This intercourse serves to keep the language somewhat uniform. Yet there are variations as one travels north. At the south, about Port Clarence and vicinity, there are many harsh, long, jaw-breaking words, while farther north there are comparatively few. The guttural, however, is present everywhere; not the liquid guttural of the German, but an intensely deep, throat-scraping one. So many Kanaka sailors have been north that several of their words have been adopted for use in trading. Whalemen who have been in Hudson's Bay and learned the native language there, have but little difficulty in conversing with Point Barrow natives. Some words are entirely different—Nakooruk, for instance—but the greater number are practically the same, differing only in a syllable or termination. Many words are found at Indian Point, Siberia, which correspond more with the Point Hope tongue than with the Masinker. In fact, there are more Nakooruk words there than at East Cape, or the Diomedes.

Some of the more common words, particularly of the region from Point Hope to Point Barrow, are the following: Man is *in-nuk;* boy is *ill-ill-e-gak;* woman is *ok-an-ok;* girl is *ok-an-ow-rok;* baby is *mick-er-o;* gun is *shoo-pung;* good is *nakooruk;* better is *na-koo-pa-yah;* best is *na-koo-pa yak-took;* the essence of perfection or goodness is *na-koo-she-ak-to.* Cold has four degrees of comparison. There are four degrees of negation. In fact, these cases of four degrees are frequent. Words with different and delicate shades of meaning are numerous. I is *oo-wung-ah;* the summer hut is *too-pick;* the winter hut is *ig-a-loo;* dog is *kig-mok;* the name of chanting to drive away the devil is *e-vu-ra-cog-a-uk-tuk;* drowsy is *e-yah-zra-rung-na;* slow is *shu-kis-hu-pe-roon-e;* fast is *shuk-i-sho-a-roon-e;* the frock, or garment, that covers the body is an *ar-tig-gi;* trousers are *co-co-leet;* water-boots are *ar-co-co-leet;* other boots are named according to the material of which they are made, or the pattern in which they are cut. In a vocabulary of eleven hundred common and useful words made by Mr. John Kelley, there are but four of one syllable.

I am told that during the winter months the natives are particular in regard to the cleanliness of their persons and their homes. This is reassuring, for in summer their persons are at the opposite extreme, judging by both sight and smell. The short summer is one great holiday, and in it the natives ignore all trouble and care, and wear out their old clothes. The demand for soap increases gradually year by

A LITTLE BROTHER AND SISTER.   Page 15.

year, as also does that for underclothing which can be washed.

Any peculiarity of person, or manner, is very quickly picked up, and most captains are designated in this way. In trying to describe an old sailor, a native put both hands to his mouth, back to, and pointed his forefingers in opposite directions, moving them slowly, showing that the man talked two ways, or, in simple English, told lies.

The tobacco habit seems to be instinctive, from the sucking babe, which frequently gets a second-hand chew from its mother, to the old people who can only munch with their toothless gums. The nicotine that collects in a much-used pipe is greatly relished, and tobacco juice is swallowed as though it were some sweetmeat. But perhaps this is from a spirit of rigid economy. A native would go a hundred miles for a supply of tobacco were he out. Whenever the jaws of the chewer get tired, the partly chewed cud is frequently laid away behind the ear like a pencil, or otherwise held over for another time. A child old enough to walk is old enough to have a pipe.

Matches are much used, yet the tinder-**box**

is always handy, especially for lighting the pipe. The old method of making a light by friction, in rubbing a piece of wood, which is fitted into a socket in another piece, the former

MAKING A LIGHT BY FRICTION.
(*From an Eskimo Drawing.*)

perpendicular, and the latter held on the ground, is still used. Bits of cotton grass which have been soaked in a solution of charcoal and water, then dried, serve as tinder.

Music, if it can be called such, is in an exceptionally elementary state. I only heard one song, but that one over and over again, a very little less than five hundred times. It was as follows:

Yung ah, yah, yung ah.   Yung ah, yah, yung ah,

and so on, with slight modifications, until the singer went to sleep or stopped from exhaustion. To hear a mother sing this soul-stirring melody to her offspring, in a voice that closely resembles a poorly played bagpipe, both in tone and shrillness, and then see her sway back and forth, and occasionally vary the rhythm by bobbing up and down as she sat Turkish fashion, or jumping a sort of a jig— well, it is not strange the infant goes to sleep. This song serves for all occasions, be they of joy or sorrow, and might be most appropriately termed the Nakooruk national hymn. But there is another song which I am told vies with it in popularity. It begins as follows:

Yah ya ko, ya ya ko,
Yah ya ko, yaw ya, ko yaw,

and ends with the same thrilling sentiment. The words of both songs are meaningless.

CHAPTER VII.

SOME TYPICAL EXPERIENCES.

To give a brief picture of Arctic whaling, vividly and picturesquely, I have gathered the following main events from participants in them.

THE WRECK OF THE BARK NAPOLEON.

The sad disaster connected with the wreck of the bark *Napoleon* has so woven itself into my narrative, and is so typical of the fate that hangs over every Arctic whaleman, that I give it as told to me by Capt. S. P. Smith, and completed by James B. Vincent, whom the *Bear* rescued.

"On the night of May 3, 1885, it blew the hardest I had ever known it to in the Arctic regions. I hove-to, as I could not keep a stitch of sail on the ship. Cape Navarin lay about fifty miles north-northeast of us. At ten minutes before seven on the evening of Tuesday the 5th, the men came out of the forecastle saying that the ship was full of water. Our only safety lay in flight, so I kept the ship off the edge of the ice so that we might have room to lower the boats. The ship soon became unmanageable, but the boats were all safely cleared away, and in less than fifteen minutes from the time we struck the cake of ice that stove us, she had capsized, not giving us time to get food or drink, or to save anything except what we stood in. Ten minutes after she went down the ice surrounded her, but we succeeded in getting near enough to get off the main royal to use in case of necessity in building a tent to protect us from the wind on the ice. That night we lay around in the ice, the wind still blowing a gale, accompanied by frequent snow-squalls. The next morning we got out of the ice and worked northeast. We had lowered all five boats, but it seemed best to divide among four, for convenience in hauling the boats over the ice.

"At noon of the next day, the weather was clear and pleasant, but at night the wind came on again with heavy snow-squalls. We endeavored to keep the boats together, but as darkness came on, the third and fourth mates got separated from us. The mate and I waited for them. Soon the third mate came up and said the fourth was near. We waited a long time, and as he did not come, concluded that something had happened to him. An hour later, we lost run of each other. I concluded that the best thing to do was to drag my boat, and to do this, I used the oars, mast, and a tub of tow-line.

"The next day, Thursday, it was still blowing heavily, and it continued through the night with snow-squalls. Friday it moderated. We made a sort of tent over the boat with the sail to keep off the water that was dashing over us. Soon afterward, however, we shipped a big sea that threatened to swamp us. About eleven o'clock I hauled in the drag, and made sail. That evening we came to a large strip of ice, and making fast to it, lay down to get what rest we could. This was the first opportunity we had had for sleep.

"Saturday morning broke clear. I aroused the men only to find that one had died. We got under way, and tried to find some of the ships, or to reach shore. About noon, we discovered what we thought to be two sails. Two hours later, the *Fleetwing* picked us up. We learned that the fourth mate and his crew had been picked up that morning about six o'clock, two of his men having died. One of the men in my boat died within five minutes after he was rescued. Most of us were frost-bitten, and our hands, feet, and legs were much swollen, but we all recovered, excepting one man who was obliged to have part of his foot amputated.

"When we left the ship all the food we had was a half-dozen, or so, cakes of ship-bread. The next day we killed two pup seals. I tried to eat some of the raw meat, but chose rather to starve. Some of the men stomached the meat.

"Later in the season I shipped as boat-header on the *Orca*, and finished the season in her."

Vincent was in the mate's boat, and taking up the narrative from the time the boats became separated, said:

"Two days after we separated from the captain's and other two boats, we fell in with the third mate. Everybody was still alive in his boat, as in ours. We determined to keep together, and endeavored to reach shore in the bight under the Cape, for that seemed our only alternative. In doing this we got caught in the ice, and were four days without food. Then we caught two young seals and divided them among the men, but there was no way of cooking, and the stomachs of many of the men were so weak that they could not keep this food down, owing to the meat being so strong and fishy. The mind of one man after another began to weaken until several were crazy. Among them was the mate, Rogers, and we were obliged to lash him down to the thwarts of the boat.

"It was thirty-six days before we reached shore. Meantime nine of the eighteen men had died and the two seals had long been eaten. The cold was terrible, and most of the men that survived were more or less frost-bitten. I was the only one that could walk when we reached shore. In a few days five more died, and the three that remained were helpless from frost-bites and exhaustion. We fell in with some natives that were fishing. Some of them lived inland, and they took me with them when they returned to their homes. My hope was to travel around the Gulf of Anadir and reach

A YOUNG WOMAN OF ABOUT EIGHTEEN   Page 159.

SOME TYPICAL EXPERIENCES. 193

Plover Bay, where I might fall in with some of the whalers. But the impossibility of this plan was soon developed, for no natives were traveling in that direction, and I could not go alone, so I remained with my newly made friends all winter.

"In the spring we returned to the shore again to fish, and my three shipmates were found barely alive. They supposed I had gone to Plover Bay, and shortly before had sent a message to the whalers through the natives, telling of their whereabouts and giving their names, but not mentioning mine. (This message was received by the Russian trading brig *Siberia*, and Captain Lincoln searched for the men on his return down the coast, but they had died before he arrived. The natives told him that Vincent was alive, but he understood them to say something about venison, as he had not heard of this name before.) I was within thirteen miles of where the *Siberia* anchored, but did not know of her presence until too late.

"After our fishing was over, we returned to the mountains again for the winter, driving our reindeer before us. Some time in midwinter—

the first of January as near as I could guess— I carved the message that was received on the bark *Hunter*, and which brought about my rescue, hardly daring to dream that it would accomplish its object. As the spring opened, we again started for the sea-shore for the usual fishing, and while there I saw a little girl with some cookies that Mrs. Simmons had given her, only a few hours before, on the *Sea Breeze*. It was too late, however, for me to get word on board, for the calm that had held the vessel was over, and she had sailed.

"No one can imagine how overjoyed I was, about ten weeks later, when my attention was attracted by the shouting of the natives, and I looked up to see a white man, and to find myself at last rescued. The officers of the revenue cutter *Bear* were exceedingly kind to me, not only while I was on board, but particularly when I landed in San Francisco, alone and penniless.

"While among the Eskimo, I was cared for by an old native whose wife received me as her son. After a year, the man died, but his last instructions to his wife were to care for, and keep me until I was rescued. When at last rescue did come, she said, with tears in her eyes, that she was ready to die, for she had done as her husband wished."

Shipwreck, starvation, freezing, or drowning are not the only dangers that threaten the sailor. Since the time that long whaling voyages were begun, desperate criminals of all sorts have taken advantage of the long absence to escape detection, and not infrequently seek new fields for their ill-trained talents. In a few instances, they have turned mutineers, and the records show all degrees of success and failure. The last experience of this kind in the Arctic fleet, as told me by Capt. Edmund Kelley, was

THE MUTINY ON STEAMER LUCRETIA.

"When master of the *Lucretia*, in 1883, I had in my crew, as I afterward found, three of the most desperate hoodlums in San Francisco, men with the worst of criminal records. I knew that the mate was not having the easiest time of it, but I was so sick and helpless with heart disease, that I dared not know too much about it. Shortly after we entered Behring Sea on our way north, the crew refused duty. A strong gale had come on, and they would not take in sail. I explained to the men how desperate their undertaking was, and the punishment for such a crime, but the three hoodlums seemed to have complete supremacy over the crew. The officers, boat-steerers, and engineers then took in sail, and we hove-to in proper shape to receive the gale. Meantime the men had retreated to the forecastle, but not before I had got the cask of ship-bread out, for I did not propose to feed mutineers. I now asked the men what their complaint was, and they replied that they hadn't any, except that they demanded the release of one of their shipmates who had been put in irons for refusal to do duty. I told them I proposed to decide for myself when the man should be released. The ringleaders then repudiated their shipping contracts, and defied me. I now had the forecastle locked up, to try the effects of starvation and meditation.

"At the close of the second day, they began quarrelling among themselves. By listening, we had learned that they had eleven revolvers, besides their knives for weapons. The next morning they broke their way out and demanded "bread or blood." I again explained to them the consequences of mutiny, endeavoring to dissuade them from going further, and told them that I would hear any complaints of ill-treatment or abuse. The cries of "bread or blood" was their only reply. I now stepped forward and said I would give them just one more chance to return to duty, but as the three ringleaders threatened to shoot the first man who wavered, no one responded.

"Taking my rifle, I deliberately walked up to the head mutineer, and demanded that he step forward and surrender. He refused. I now made a movement to cock my rifle, and as I did so, he snapped a revolver in my face twice, then ran behind the try-works. I gave chase into the midst of the mutineers. The rascal went around the try-works, came up behind me, took deliberate aim, and fired. Thinking the shot fatal, the officers and men aft fired upon him, wounding him in the leg. He dragged himself around the other way to get another shot at me, but I met him, took good aim and fired, putting a ball through his heart. He dropped dead.

"I now turned about for the next ringleader, and was surprised to see revolvers and knives going overboard and the men all running for the forecastle. I called every man back on deck. As they came up they begged mercy, the two ringleaders beseeching me piteously not to shoot them. All were very willing to return to work. They offered no excuses further than that they had been misled and misguided. During the rest of the season they were as good a crew as there was in the fleet. I had to leave the ship on account of my health, but just before I left, most of the men, of their own accord, drew up a paper entirely exonerating me, and signed it. When I arrived in San Francisco I reported the affair to the Federal Court, and, after hearing the evidence, the judge censured me for not shooting the other two ringleaders, then discharged me."

Wind and ice have caused a large majority of the disasters in the Arctic. Such disasters, however, are inevitable. But the raid of the rebel cruiser *Shenandoah* was wanton destructiveness. Here is the story of it, and its great cost to ship-owners.

THE RAID OF THE SHENANDOAH.

Captain Bauldry was first mate of the ship *Addison* when the *Shenandoah* appeared to the Arctic whaling fleet in June, 1865. "The *Brunswick*," said he, "had been stove while in the vicinity of Plover Bay, and we, with several other ships, went to her assistance. Later in the same day, we kept off Cape Thaddeus. On the second day afterward, I think it was, we saw smoke, and soon a long black steamer hove in sight. We supposed it to be in the employ of the company then preparing to lay a telegraph cable between Asia and America, and proposed to run down and speak it, to learn the late news; but a strip of ice two miles wide lay between us, so we continued cruising, intending to return soon. A thick fog set in and we saw no more. When it cleared up a trifle, I saw, from aloft, heavy smoke in the direction of those ships. We were surprised, for we knew they had no whales when we left, and they had not had time to get any and get to boiling.

"The next day we had turned back. I called the captain's attention to what appeared to be a log-book floating on the water, and as we advanced we came upon more wreckage, but even then it did not enter our heads who the stranger was, or what had happened. We followed along, picking up oars, gear, etc. The next morning the *Canton Packet* came down under full sail and signaled us. We hauled aback, and Captain Allen told us who the stranger was, and that he was burning up the whole fleet. Afterward the *Jireh Perry* came down under full sail. The cruiser had chased her, but there was a good breeze and she was too fleet for him. We had been following in the wake of the *Shenandoah* as fast as sail could carry us, but now we turned about, and in company with the two vessels, went south to St. Paul's Island, then skirted the Alaskan shore closely, working north. Two or three days after we went south, the *General Pike* came along and spoke us. She had been bonded, and with two hundred and fifty men on board, crews from burned ships, was bound for San Francisco. We were then told that the whole fleet had been burned up.

NAKOORUK WITH LABRET.—Page 169.

"We had all heard of the fall of Richmond, and several captains had told Waddell of it, but he was not prepared to believe it, he said, and so continued his depredations. But in the Straits a Dutch trader, that had just come up, showed him late papers, assuring him of the fall of the Confederacy. This was on the 28th of July. He then went across the Straits from East Cape to Cape Prince of Wales, firing guns, but attacking nobody. As he headed south on the east shore, we sailed into the Arctic close under the west shore. He had burned most of the finest ships in the fleet.

"When the cruiser bore down on the *Brunswick*, Captain Potter sent a boat aboard to tell of his crippled condition and ask assistance. Waddell replied that he would soon give him all the assistance necessary, then proceeded to burn all the ships in sight. Among them was the *Favorite*, of Fairhaven, Mass., Capt. James G. Young. When he saw what was up, Captain Young prepared to defend himself. All the fire-arms were brought out, and he mounted the house, bomb-gun in hand, but the first mate saw that resistance was useless and quietly removed all the caps. As the *Shenandoah's* boat was coming on its incendiary errand, Captain Young raised the bomb-gun and ordered it off. It continued coming, and he snapped his gun, intending to blow the boat to atoms. When he found what the mate had done, he could do nothing but submit. When the lieutenant in the boat came on board he accosted the captain and said: ' Would you have shot me?' ' Shot you!' was the reply, 'yes, shot you like a dog!' Though nearly seventy years old, his inhuman captors put the courageous old man in irons and imprisoned him in their coal bunkers.

"After we had escaped, we feared capture every day, and prepared for it. I had about $250 in English sovereigns, which I concealed in holes bored in the soles and heels of my boots. I put a few other valuables in my pillow. When the *General Williams* was captured, Captain Benjamin carried $600 in his hand, but his captors promptly relieved him of it.

"Before entering Behring Sea, the *Shenandoah* had invaded the Ochotsk, where several vessels were burned, among them the *Abagail*, Capt. Ebenezer Nye. Captain Nye immedi ately set out with two whale-boats to warn the Arctic fleet of the approaching danger, and through this act, several ships were enabled to escape. The second mate of the *Abagail*, named Manning, was a Southerner, and he, with a renegade Northerner named Dowden, piloted the rebel into the Arctic. Dowden has never courted the society of the whalemen since.

"The cruiser burned thirty vessels, and bonded four. New Bedford's loss alone was twenty-three vessels, which, with their outfits, were valued at $1,000,000. The prospective catch was another million."

The first great set-back to Arctic whaling was the wreck season of 1871. While I was with Capt. Edmund Kelley he told me the story of it, as follows:

THE GREAT WRECK SEASON OF 1871.

"On August 6, 1871, five of us ships worked between the ice-pack and the shoals off Icy Cape. The shore was five miles off, while the edge of the pack extended in nearly a straight line from the Cape to Wainwright Inlet. As the ice opened, we worked northeast, whaling all the time, till we reached the end of the open water. There we made fast to the pack. Many other sails followed behind us. On the 11th,

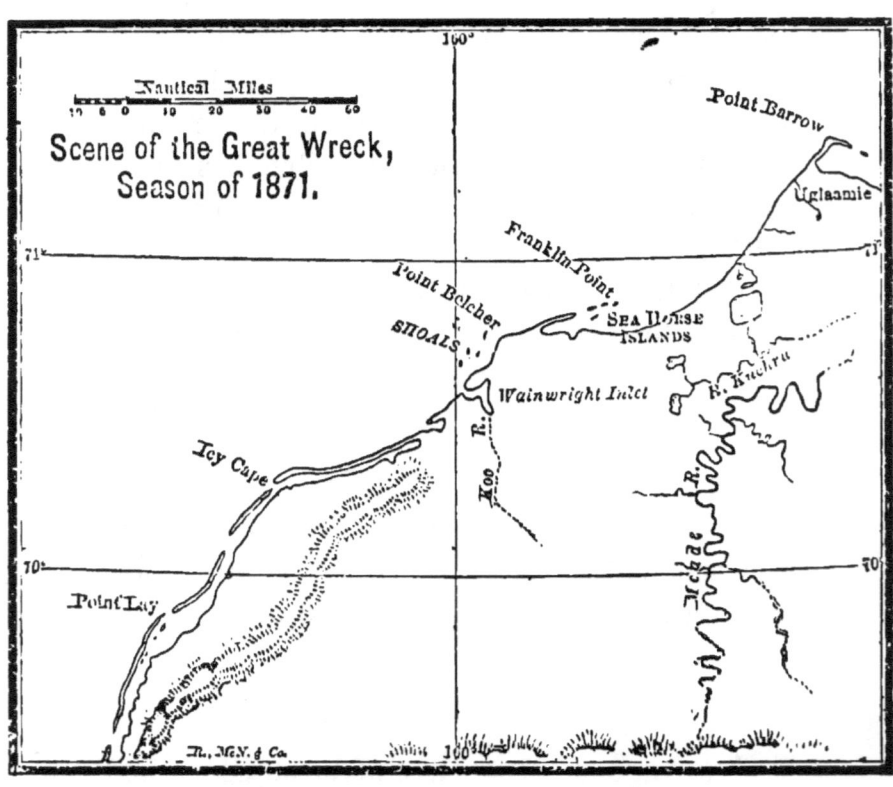

we had an opportunity to lower the boats, but the ice closed up suddenly, and we were forced to drag twenty-six boats over it. Fourteen boats were collected on a single cake at one

SOME TYPICAL EXPERIENCES. 205

time. Within half an hour from the time the ice began to move, we were solidly inclosed. On the 13th, we were twenty sails, part of us beset in the ice, others riding at anchor. The 16th brought thirteen more ships. The next day a movement in the ice forced us to haul up anchor, and get nearer in-shore. We were all on the outside edge of the shoals extending from near Wainwright Inlet to Point Belcher. I determined to get inside the shoals; so, with a lead, I picked out a channel across them, and marked it by sinking bundles of bricks to which were attached pieces of wood to act as buoys. The other ships followed in my wake, and we all got inside, although two ships went ashore in doing so. On the 29th, we lay within three-quarters of a mile of the shore. By this time the pack had reached the shoals. The next day thirty-two ships were fast in the ice. I was stowing down oil, and allowed no thought of danger to enter my head. On the first day of September the *Roman* was carried off in the pack. The next day came the news that she and the brig *Comet* were crushed. The current now set in slow, and the ice began to pack. As a precautionary measure, Capt. Tom Williams and I went south, searching for open water, but it was in vain. We felt that there was no possibility of rescue, yet, at every opportunity, we kept on whaling, as deliberately as though we expected to get out the next day. But we were anxious, and meetings of all the captains were held nearly every day, and every phase of the situation thoroughly discussed. Just north of Wainwright Inlet was the trading brig *Victoria*, and I was commissioned to see if I could not get her over the shoals. Meantime, Capt. David Frazer, with two whale-boats, had been sent south to see what he could do. In two days he returned and reported that the rest of the fleet, seven ships, were fast in the ice north of Icy Cape, but that they would stand by the other ships. Getting out of their predicament in a few days, they lay at anchor waiting developments. We captains were still holding meetings, for we felt keenly our responsibility, with $3,000,000 worth of property, and twelve hundred lives at stake. Young ice formed nearly every night, and the land was covered with snow. There was every indication that winter had set in.

"Finally, on the 13th, it was resolved to

abandon the fleet the next day if there was no change. Some time before this, the women and children, with quantities of provisions, had been sent to the ships below. Meantime, three other ships, the *Eugenia*, *Julian* and *Awashonk*, had been crushed, and all their provisions lost. Their crews were rescued, and divided up among the other ships. With terrible suspense and anxiety, we waited for the next day, September 14th. When it did come, there was the same weather, and a motionless barometer. Accordingly, signals were set, each whale-boat manned by its crew, and the journey to the ships ninety miles south begun. Thirty-three ships, some of them as fine as any ever built, were abandoned, or already wrecked. The sad procession of our two hundred, or so, whale-boats wound its way through a narrow strip of water between the ice and the shore, bottom often being struck, it was so shallow. Young ice had frequently to be broken to get through. At night we encamped on the shore, and the next morning we resumed our journey, getting on board the ships that afternoon. There were not accommodations for more than forty men on board any of these ships, yet in addition to their own crews, and the women and children, they had to divide up these twelve hundred men. Sail was immediately made. Port was made at Honolulu, only seven of the splendid fleet of forty vessels that had left that port less than a year before returning. But not a life had been lost.

"When the ships were abandoned, all liquors, and whatever might be an evil to the natives, were destroyed. Hardly had we stepped from the ships, when the natives, who were camped along the shore in hopes of plunder, took possession and helped themselves. One sailor, whose mind was not right, deserted the night we camped, and returned to the fleet. He hoped to save the whalebone, be rescued the next season, and thus make his fortune; but the natives not only took the bone from him, but threatened to murder him. When rescued the next season, the sailor told of the plundering of the ships by the natives. We had not destroyed our medicine chests at the abandonment, for we knew there was a possibility of our having to return again. The natives were cautioned against touching these chests, but without avail, and a number were poisoned by

A TEAM OF DOGS AND DOG SLEDGES.—Page 177.

drinking the medicines. Out of superstitious dread, every ship on which a native was poisoned, was burned. The next season, my ship, the *Seneca*, and the *Minerva* were found to be in good condition. The former was lost in an attempt to save her, but the other was saved and again went into service.

"I had a big St. Bernard dog on my ship, and he seemed to fully comprehend the situation. When it came to leaving the ship, I got the boats away, then returned to take a parting look at the cabin. The dog followed me, although I never before had allowed him below. As I put a needle in the clock to stop it at the hour of parting, the dog put his forepaws on the table before me, and looked me clearly in the eye with a most intelligent expression. 'Bos,' said I, 'we must leave the ship.' He cried pitifully. When I returned on deck, he followed. Heavy and clumsy as he was, he gave himself up completely, and we lowered him into the boat with perfect ease."

Following closely on the horror of 1871 came the disaster of 1876, much more dreadful, with its great loss of life. Capt. Wm. H.

Kelley, who lost the *Marengo*, gave me the following account of it:

THE HORROR OF 1876.

"Early in August we reached Point Barrow, in spite of heavy ice. Soon we began whaling, but the constantly moving ice, and strong currents, made it very dangerous, though whales were numerous. Finally, the pack came down on the north side of the Point, driving the ships south. The wind shifted into the southeast, causing the pack to close in rapidly. At this, we made the fatal mistake of attempting to beat south against a strong northeast current. When it was too late, we saw our mistake, but kept persevering. Working down into a deep pocket in the ice, we found ourselves being closed in upon, and after ten hours of hard beating, were completely beset. Two of the smaller vessels got well in-shore and escaped, while two vessels had remained at anchor. We at the south were solidly held in the moving pack. All navigation was ended and we were entirely at the mercy of the ice, drifting slowly but surely into the northeast. Immense ice jams wound themselves about the ships, choking up every avenue of escape. Some of the ice-floes were miles in extent. I had never seen such ice before, and each succeeding day increased the barrier.

"At last we came to an apparent standstill. We masters held frequent meetings. Cold weather was fast approaching and a number of ships had narrowly escaped being nipped by the ice. Seeing no hope of escape, I began to seriously consider the best means of saving my crew. Two boats were made ready to haul over the ice in case we had to abandon the ship, for this was our only hope of escape.

"Finally, at a meeting of the masters in my cabin, it was decided that if there were no change for the better within a certain time, we would abandon the ships. Clothing and provisions were portioned out to each man, to be ready. The hour came without a sign of a change. I was asked to be the pilot. The crews were marshaled on the ice, each ship's company with two boats, shod, to stand hauling over the ice. Some of the men positively refused to leave their ships. The boats would be hauled half a mile or more over the ice, then we would return for the clothing and provisions.

Then the boats would be dragged another half mile and the packs brought up. Thus we kept on until darkness interfered, and we camped on a large ice-floe that night. We made our camp by turning the boats over, crawling under them, and lying down on the ice to get what sleep we could. Before morning there was a heavy snow-storm and day dawned thick and gloomy. After a hasty breakfast of salt pork and hard bread, we again took up the march. I fell into the water twice while picking out the best track, and nearly froze to death, but by breaking up one of the small boats and building a fire, I dried my clothes and got rested. Then we started on again. The close of the second day found us encamped on a large cake of ice that was grounded in twelve fathoms of water. The following night was even more gloomy than the preceding one had been. All open holes of water were frozen over—a warning that we must lose no time. Again we made our beds upon the ice. It was one of the most miserable nights I ever experienced.

"At daybreak we started again, launching our boats. The young ice that had formed was not strong enough to bear us, so we had to break our way through for several hundred yards, when we reached a floe. Then we hauled the boats over this. At noon we stopped to eat something, but self-denial was necessary in order that our scanty supply of provisions might hold out as long as possible. I crawled to the top of the highest iceberg at hand and swept the horizon with my glass. Seeing land in the far distance, I cried 'Land, ho!' and it was re-echoed by hundreds of voices. The journey was now resumed with renewed energy. At about three o'clock we came upon a great crevasse, which was fully twenty feet broad and twelve or fifteen feet deep. This extended a long distance each way and lay directly across our course. To go around would consume a great deal of time, so we formed a bridge of our boats and thus passed over. At seven in the evening we reached the narrow strip of water next to the land. The boats were now launched, and for the first time we set our sails. By ten o'clock we reached shore. Stores were unloaded, and in less than fifteen minutes the beach was lined with fires. The boats were hauled up high and dry, then the tired and exhausted men, whom no prudence could restrain, ate a hearty meal and lay down for such sleep as they could get.

"There was now a fair prospect of escape, yet our salvation lay with the ships below Point Barrow. At daybreak all were aroused. Provisions were low, but the sailors, with their usual improvidence, ate as if they had a year's supply on hand. Boats were launched, and, in the face of a freezing wind, we got under way. We rowed some time, but the men suffered so much from cold, that we landed and towed the boats along the beach, canal-boat fashion. By this exercise we kept up a circulation of blood. The moisture of our breaths froze on our whiskers, forming bundles of ice that looked like the old-fashioned dipped candles. When we had made about fifteen miles in this way, we came to shore-ice and had to take to the boats.

"That night we camped on the beach and met some natives. They begged all they could from us, and otherwise showed disregard for our pitiable condition. Probably it was our numbers that kept them from other imposition, perhaps robbery. The next day, the fifth, the wind had died out and the weather was intensely cold, so that young ice formed rapidly. Still we pushed on, breaking our way through as best we could. But the nearer we drew to Point Barrow, the thicker the ice became. When within two miles of it, we landed on a low sand-spit and shot a number of wild ducks, and the starving men greedily devoured them, so that those who shot them got nothing. From here on, it was difficult getting along, but at last we reached the ships, and were kindly received. A consultation was held, and it was deemed best for us to continue our journey to Cape Smyth.

"On the evening of the next day we reached bark *Florence* and were most cordially received by the Captains Williams, one of whose vessels was six miles below. Both ships lay in comparative safety behind ground-ice. Each captain offered us the shelter of his vessel, and a share of the last biscuit on board, should it become necessary.

"We concluded that the open sea could not be reached without destruction to the boats, for the solid pack lay on the shore as far south as Icy Cape, and there was no open water along the land. This left only the alternative of waiting where we were, in hopes that a gale would come up, drive the ice off-shore, and set the ships free. As a precautionary measure, and to consume time and attention, we began to build winter quarters on shore, while the best whalemen were picked out to catch whales, and thus lay in a winter's supply of food. The remaining men were told off into gangs, some to gather wood, others to gather turf to cover the hut. Were no whales caught, starvation was inevitable, and were no protection from the elements prepared, freezing to death was inevitable. Everybody worked with a will, and the hut soon assumed shape. The men lived in tents of old sail-cloth.

"On the first day of our work a light breeze sprang up. The next day it increased to a gale. With each increasing gust our hopes rose accordingly. On the third day the gale had so increased that the ice began to move. Slowly but surely it drew back, leaving only the ground cakes, behind which the ships lay.

"While we were busily working on the fourth day, the signal was given that escape was possible. With a shout, work was abandoned, and a wild rush made for the boats.

Pell-mell the men tumbled into them, even forgetting the few articles they still possessed, and leaving the tents standing. It took but a few minutes to get the whole fleet of boats under way, bound toward the *Florence*. Our stock of provisions was almost exhausted and we had been on allowance for some time. Starvation was staring us in the face. When we arrived, we found that Captain Williams had succeeded in cutting a passage through the ice and had anchored his vessel outside a large ground cake. As soon as we all got aboard, anchor was weighed, and we ran down to the *Clara Bell*. She was fast in the ice, so she was abandoned, and her crew came aboard the *Florence*.

"On our way south we stopped at Wainwright Inlet for some wood, and while there were joined by the *Three Brothers*. Half the men were put on board her, and after appointing a rendezvous, we separated. We met as agreed, made a final division of men and provisions, each taking half. When we entered the Golden Gate the last piece of meat was in the copper, and the last loaf of bread in the oven. Thus we barely made ends meet.

"Not a particle was ever seen of the abandoned ships nor a word ever heard from the one hundred and fifty men that remained on board of them."

In most seasons it is a terrible ordeal to get out of the Arctic safely. With gales, currents, blinding snow-storms, and long, dark nights, each master has literally to feel his way with the lead, and get what aid he can with log and lookout. As typical of what this ordeal is, also of what dangers the Arctic navigator is called upon to go through, I give

THE EXPERIENCES OF CAPTAIN BAULDRY.

"When master of the ship *Navy*, in 1870, I got caught in a heavy gale and thick snow-storm that began on the third of October and lasted thirteen days. I supposed myself on the Alaskan shore, but when it cleared up, I found myself off Cape Serge, Siberia, and it was with great difficulty that we kept from going ashore. Driven over into the vicinity of "Big" River, as we call the Koliutchin River, I sought the lee of the island of the same name, and dropped anchor. Between the island and the main land was a tide rip where the breakers rose high in the air, leading us to fear that we were running directly on a sand-bar. Yet we could do nothing else but risk it. Had it been one, every man would have been drowned. All the sails had been blown away by the gale, and nearly all hands were frost-bitten. Fearing that we would have to spend the winter here, I went ashore to a settlement of natives to see what the prospects were. Meantime new sails were bent to be ready, should the wind haul and give us a chance to get out. On the 16th the wind began to slacken, but, as it did so, the northwest pack moved down on us. Nevertheless, we got under way. Then young ice began to form, and it was so thick that we could hardly press through it. Finally, however, we emerged into clear water, and on the 18th passed through the Straits.

"The same gale had played havoc with the rest of the fleet. The *Japan*, Capt. F. A. Barker, had been carried ashore at East Cape and wrecked· and the *Massachusetts*, Captain Cody, would also have been wrecked had not the other disaster been witnessed by all hands, who did not suspect the presence of land.

Several other ships also suffered from the gale. Had I known of the wreck of the *Japan*, I might have hauled in under East Cape, taken all on board, and saved them from wintering there.

"With such an experience as this, and so narrow an escape from being wrecked, I looked forward to a good passage down, but in this I was greatly mistaken. Off St. Matthew's Island a sea struck us, breaking off the cutwater, carrying away the bob-stays, and generally wrecking the stem. I soon patched things up, but we had hardly recovered before we encountered another gale off St. Paul's Island. There we were struck by a sea that carried away all the boats and davits on the port side, and stove the bulwarks all round. We looked to be thoroughly smashed up, but arrived safely at Honolulu without further mishap of consequence.

"The next year I lost the *Navy* in the great wreck, when the thirty-three ships were abandoned.

"In 1873, when I had the *Arnolda*, I had a much narrower escape from being wrecked than I had in 1870. Early in October, when off Point Barrow, I stove in one bow, breaking four planks and four timbers. To press it back into place, it was necessary to cut off three more timbers. I was advised to abandon the ship, but declined to leave her until I was obliged to. By the time I got the last timber cut off the hold was full and the water had reached the between-decks. We had the blubber of three whales on board, so that the main hatches could not be got at to bail out and aid the pumps: but by working in the water, I got a tarred blanket over the break, then put boards over, and, with spars, wedged the bow back into place. Had she not been a live-oak ship, the pressure on the other bow would have broken that out. To add to the confusion, the boat-steerers got at a keg of rum, and all were dead drunk when I got on deck.

"In this crippled condition, I went down to Plover Bay, and there, by the aid of Capt. W. H. Kelley, and others, got the bow out of water, filled up the cracks with sawdust, put on tarred canvas, then planked it all over. Thus a check was put on the leak. We got out of Behring Sea all right, but just below the Aleutian

Islands encountered a gale which threatened to swamp us. It would have done so had it lasted long, for the leak gained on us, though the pumps were going all the time. When we arrived at Honolulu we were leaking 20,000 strokes in twenty-four hours. To put the planking on, I had used six-inch spikes, but when we reached port they were eaten down as small as ten-penny nails. The ship carpenter who repaired her said they could not have lasted a week longer, and it was a wonder they held as long as they did. The next year I stove her stem so that she leaked 22,000 strokes in twenty-four hours on the way down.

"But there has been no experience in the Arctic that equals what I went through with in 1879 when I had the *Helen Mar*. The weather held good, and, as there was whaling, several of us stayed late. We were in the vicinity of Herald Island, and, as there were no indications of ice, we felt safe. One by one the vessels kept off until only four of us remained. I knew it was not safe to remain longer, for one night's freezing might hold us there for good; so I ran down to the *Mercury*, telling Captain Hickmott that I was bound out.

He had just picked up a dead whale, and asked me to wait till he got it cut in, then we could go out together. That night, the 23d of October, we saw in the distance the 'bug light' of the *Mt. Wollaston*, Capt. Ebenezer Nye. Near him was the *Vigilant*, Capt. Chas. R. Smethers, and that was the last ever seen of them.

"In running out I wanted to go by Herald Shoals, but Captain Hickmott thought a better route would be by Cape Serge. When we came to young ice off the Cape, I knew it was of no use going further, so we kept off for the Shoals; but there, too, we were now headed off. The northwest pack had come down, and the north pack had been driven south so that both rested on the Shoals. Here we were in a large hole, so large that a ship could go on one tack all day long, yet we were hemmed in. The ice was fast moving north, so I let go both anchors with ninety fathoms of cable, hoping to hold the vessel and let the ice drift by. The *Mercury* was made fast to my stern by hawsers. This proved futile, and we drifted off into the northeast with the ice.

"A fierce northeast gale now sprang up, lasting six hours. The *Mercury* made all sail, but was caught hopelessly in the ice. I was in a better position, and, as it was evident that the chances were against our getting out, it was decided to abandon her, as my vessel was stronger and more seaworthy. That night young ice formed that would hold a ton of blubber and fifteen men. Though the *Mercury's* last whale was a dead one, we knew that, as a last resort, the blubber could be depended upon for food, so we dragged it across the ice with all the provisions, and put everything aboard my ship. This took four days, and just as we got the last article moved and everybody safely on board, my ship began to move. I had never before imagined such cold as we now experienced. We had a fire in the forecastle, two in the blubber room, and one in the cabin, yet every night frost an inch or more thick would form on the inside of the ship. A timely gale from the northwest broke the ice sufficiently for me to feel a faint ray of hope ahead, though no open water could be seen from the masthead. We cut ourselves free from the *Mercury* and made all sail. We could only steer with the sails, as the rudder was held solid by ice. The stem was a mass of solid ice even to the catheads, and around the ship at the water's edge was a regular platform of ice, so that one could walk around the vessel.

"The gale pressed us forward into the ice, and we ran all night through heavy ice, headed, as near as we could judge, for Point Hope. The next day the ice grew lighter, so that we made more headway.

"After two days and two nights we came into clear water. Here another gale struck us, and it was the most terriffic one I had ever experienced at sea. Coming from the northeast, it brought heavy ice-floes down on us, and we had these to contend against as well as the fear of running ashore. So much 'ice-smoke' rose from the water that nothing could be seen ahead of us from the deck, so I stationed myself in the foretop and remained there till the gale subsided, directing the ship as best I could, and keeping clear of the largest pieces of ice. The next day the weather moderated and we reached the Diomedes. No human being can imagine what we had gone through, or what anxiety of mind I suffered with all these lives dependent upon me. Neither the mate, Mr. Carter, or myself had had a bit of sleep for five nights or days, and I feared he would die, he was so nervous. To induce sleep, I gave him a large amount of laudanum, and he lay with both eyes wide open, yet in the deepest sleep. Had there been fifteen miles more of ice to go through, we certainly would have gone to the bottom. The ship could not have stood the strain. As it was, she was almost cut through on the bluff of both bows. The ice had been fearful. It seems as if we must have been mysteriously guided past the large pieces, for had we struck one solidly, it would have sunk us. Gold whales and a gold ship would not tempt me to undergo another such experience.

"The gale let go, and we were waiting to pass through the Straits. At that moment a breeze from the south sprang up and opened the way in the barrier of ice. We started to beat down, and, giving the course to the officer on deck, I lay down for my first rest in apparent security. But in the night the wind shifted, and while we were going ahead at the rate of six knots an hour, headed south-southeast, with the wind, the current was carrying us astern into the north-northeast at the rate of three knots. At three o'clock in the morning, during a thick snow-squall, the ship struck bottom. I felt the first thump, and, comprehending the situation, rushed on deck. Before I got there the men had hauled down all the sails and were throwing things overboard to lighten the ship. I got all sail on her again, hove her on her beam ends, and floated her off. When daylight came we got out of the current and beyond all these dangers. We had struck on the shoals off Cape Prince of Wales, and the marvel is that it did not complete the work the ice had so well begun, and taken the bottom off the ship. As it was, she left her false keel and forefoot there. None of us could have lived to reach shore in that sea of icy water; or, if any had lived through it, the treacherous natives on the Cape would probably have ended our lives. Captain Hickmott's wife and young daughter were prepared to drown themselves rather than attempt to reach shore.

"The wheel could only be moved two spokes when we finally got out, owing to ice in the rudder-box. That south wind alone rescued us. Had it come a few hours earlier, we could not possibly have escaped, and its short duration is probably what caused the loss of the other two ships. It was the first of November when we finally left the Arctic, the latest that any ship has ever come out. To think that we had gone through such a terrible ordeal then to run ashore, was disheartening, but after once fairly homeward bound, sailing was comparatively smooth. We had plenty of provisions for the seventy-three persons on board, but toward the last the fresh water ran short, and each person was limited to three pints a day. We had been given up for lost by everybody at home, for we were nearly a month late. When we were running out through the ice it made such a noise scraping against the side of the ship that we could not hear one speak in a loud voice, even in the cabin.

"While the men were hauling the blubber and provisions across the ice from the *Mercury*, hardened old salts as they were, they would get down on their knees, cry like children, and pray to God to only deliver them, and they would be better men; but I noticed that just as soon as we were out of our troubles they gave vent to a great deal of pent-up irreverence and profanity. I never heard such swearing equaled.

"The next year the natives at Cape Serge reported that two wrecked vessels came down in a floe in the winter and that they went on board and found all hands frozen to death. From the relics they got there can be no doubt but that they saw the *Mt. Wollaston* and *Vigilant*. I am confident that I saw one of them fifteen miles, or so, off in the pack in the vicinity of Herald Island the next season, but it was impossible to reach her."

To illustrate what the life of a trader among the Eskimo is, and also to show the hospitable, yet vindictive, character of the natives, I give

CAPTAIN COGAN'S WINTER AT ST. LAWRENCE BAY, SIBERIA.

"The whaler and trader *Kohola*, of Honolulu, came north in 1862 to winter under charge of Captain Brummerhoff. I came up as first mate and navigator, intending to go down in the fall and return in the spring, but I decided to stay over, too. We wintered about a quarter of a mile from the north shore in St. Lawrence Bay, near the spot where the *Rogers* was afterward burned. Soon after we anchored the sailors went ashore, stole some whisky from one of the native huts, got drunk, and came aboard and resolved to take the ship. We put them in irons and under guard. The native of whom they stole the liquor came aboard afterward and remained two or three days. Meantime a strong gale sprang up. Some of the sailors told him they had seen the wind carry off his hut and destroy everything. This set the fellow crazy. He insisted upon going ashore. We knew it would be impossible to land him, and tried in vain to dissuade him. While we were at dinner one day, he jumped overboard and started to swim ashore. I threw a line to him, but he brushed it away and started off. He had almost reached shore, when he encountered young ice, lost his strength and was drowned, his body never being seen again. After the gale subsided, his father and two brothers came aboard inquiring for him. We told them the truth, but the sailors, who sought revenge on the captain, told them that the captain had stabbed him and thrown the body overboard. They ignored our story and believed this. They then told the captain they would kill him if he ever came ashore. On account of this affair, cheating in trade, giving poor rum mixed with pepper, etc., a strong hatred naturally sprang up among all the natives against him, and they refused to come aboard and trade. I then got a dog team by purchasing a dog here and there, learned to drive them, and started out on trading expeditions, making two as far north as East Cape and one down to Indian Point and Plover Bay.

"The farther inland I went on my expeditions the more hospitably I was received, although there was never anything left undone for my comfort. So the winter passed. Some natives lived aboard the ship, and through them, and by my expeditions, considerable trade was picked up. We had plenty of deer meat all the time from the natives, but some of the Kanaka sailors refused to take exercise or proper care of themselves, consequently were stricken with scurvy and died. While I was on one of my expeditions, the captain traded for six deer. The natives took their trade—a keg of rum—in advance, and went ashore to get the deer, which were inland. I returned at this juncture, and the captain asked me to go and get the deer; but when I found what trade he had given them, I suggested that we wait until the liquor and its effects had disappeared. He then said he would go himself, and, in spite of warnings from the rest of us and the friendly natives, he started off. We followed him with the glass and soon saw there was trouble. We could see the team returning in great haste and a crowd following. Afterward we learned that the friends of the man that had been drowned and a few other natives, incensed at the captain's treatment of them, had followed his team and sought revenge. The captain fired at them with his revolver, then threw it away and fled toward the ship, but was soon overtaken, pierced by an arrow, and then stabbed to death. I endeavored to recover the body, but could not find a trace of it, the natives saying that it had been given to the dogs; but I recovered his clothing. The murderers then endeavored to induce all the natives along the coast to join in an attempt to seize the ship, but the plot never came to a head.

"When the natives returned to their huts after the crime, they packed up everything, and, driving their deer before them, disappeared. As the command of the ship now devolved upon me, I offered a large reward to anybody who would bring one of the murderers near enough for me to get a shot at him. This offer made it unsafe for us to venture ashore, but we received considerable more trade by it being brought aboard to us. When the whaling season opened I made sail.

"Each year afterward, as I returned north, I renewed my reward for a shot at one of the murderers, simply for effect, in case it should be necessary for others to winter there. After several years had elapsed, the wives of two fellow-masters asked me to go ashore and show them the native huts, but we had not more than landed when the two brothers of the drowned man came running toward me with big knives ready for use; but I kept them at a distance with a revolver until we reached a safe distance. The father and one of the brothers were afterward frozen to death while journeying to the Ochotsk. Twelve years after the murder the remaining brother sent word to me, asking that peace be declared. I agreed, and he came aboard to see me the next day. Four years ago, while drunk, this fellow went through the settlement with his rifle, shooting into each hut as he passed it. In one he narrowly missed shooting a little girl, and her twelve-year-old brother seized a rifle and shot him dead."

[THE END.]

Special Books for Sportsmen.

Angler's Guide Book, The, and Tourist's Gazetteer of the Fishing Waters of the United States and Canada. Compiled and edited by WILLIAM C. HARRIS, editor of the "American Angler." 8vo, 249 pages; cloth, $1.00.

The Rand-McNally Official Railway Guide and Handbook. Published monthly by the American Railway Guide Co., with official corrections and revisions to date. Complete, compact and convenient. Accompanied by Rand, McNally & Co.'s Official Railway Map of the United States, Canada and Mexico, and an index to all important railway stations in those countries. Price, per number, 25 cents.

Where the Trout Hide. By KIT CLARKE. Illustrated. Containing also a detailed description of a newly opened, easily accessible, and beautiful country, whose waters teem with brook trout, black bass, and land-locked salmon. 16mo, cloth, $1.00; paper, 50 cents.

Wild Fowl Shooting. Their resorts, habits, flight, and most successful method of hunting. By WILLIAM BRUCE LEFFINGWELL. Illustrated. Cloth, $2.50; half morocco, $3.50.

"There is not a book which could have been written that was needed by sportsmen more than one on wild fowl shooting, and one could not have been written which would have covered the subject, in all its points, more thoroughly."—*American Field.*

Indexed Pocket Maps of every State and Territory in the Union, and of each of the Canadian Provinces, showing in detail the entire railroad system, and locating every station and post office. Each, 25 cents.

Send for complete list of maps and guides.

RAND, MCNALLY & CO.,
PUBLISHERS,
CHICAGO AND NEW YORK.

Cruisings in the Cascades

AND OTHER HUNTING ADVENTURES.

A narrative of Travel, Exploration, Amateur Photography, Hunting and Fishing, with Special Chapters on Hunting the Grizzly Bear, the Buffalo, Elk, Antelope, Rocky Mountain Goat, and Deer; also on Trouting in the Rocky Mountains; on a Montana Roundup; Life Among the Cowboys, etc.

By G. O. SHIELDS ("Coquina"),

AUTHOR OF

"Rustlings in the Rockies." "Hunting in the Great West."
"The Battle of the Big Hole," Etc.

The Most Fascinating Book on Big Game Hunting Ever Published.

No sportsman's library is complete without this, "Coquina's" best production; while as a narrative of travel and adventure for the ordinary reader it is unsurpassed.

12mo; 300 pages, profusely illustrated; with handsome gold side stamp and back stamp.

PRICES:

Cloth .... $2.00.
Half Morocco .... 3.00.

Sent postpaid to any address on receipt of price.

RAND, McNALLY & CO., Publishers,

148 TO 154 MONROE ST., CHICAGO.
323 BROADWAY, NEW YORK.

GUIDE BOOKS.

BAEDEKER'S GUIDES.

The Eastern Alps, including the Bavarian Highlands, the Tyrol, Salzkammergut, Styria, Carinthia, Carniola, and Istria	$2.50
England, Wales, and Scotland, as far as Loch Maree and the Cromarty Firth	3 75
London and Its Environs, including Excursions to Brighton, the Isle of Wight, etc.	2.50
The Rhine, from Rotterdam to Constance	2.50
Belgium and Holland	2 00
Northern Germany	2.50
Southern Germany and Austria, including Hungary and Transylvania	2.50
Paris and Its Environs	2.50
Central Italy and Rome	2.50
Northern Italy, including Leghorn, Florence, Ravenna, the Island of Corsica, and routes through France, Switzerland, and Austria	2.50
Southern Italy and Sicily, with Excursions to the Lipari Islands, Malta, Sardinia, Tunis, and Corfu	2.50
Norway and Sweden	3.00
Switzerland, and the adjacent portions of Italy, Savoy, and the Tyrol	2.75
The Travelers' Manual of Conversation, in four languages—English, French, German, and Italian	1.25
Palestine and Syria	7.50
Lower Egypt, with the Fayum and the Peninsula of Sinai	5.50

MISCELLANEOUS GUIDES.

Murray's Handbook for Travelers in Ireland	$4.00
France. By the author of "Mademoiselle Mori," etc.	1.25
The Land of Greece. Described and illustrated by Chas. Henry Hanson	4.00
Florence. By Augustus J. C. Hare	1.00
Walks in Rome. By Augustus J. C. Hare	3.50
The Maritime Provinces (Canada). Osgood	1.50
All Round Route and Panoramic Guide (Hudson, St. Lawrence, Niagara, etc.) By C. R. Chisholm	1.50
The Thousand Islands. By F. B. Hough	1.25
General Guide to the United States and Canada. 2 Vols. Part I.—Eastern States and Canada; Part II.—Western and Southern States. Each	1.25
Rand, McNally & Co.'s Guide to the Pacific Coast, California, Arizona, New Mexico, Colorado, and Kansas. Paper, .75; cloth	1.00
A Week in Chicago. Profusely illustrated	.25
Pictoral Guide of Chicago. With folded map and many illustrations	.25
Guide Book for Mt. Desert. By Mrs. Clara Barnes	1.00
Rand, McNally & Co.'s Illustrated Guide to Niagara Falls	.25
Official Guide to the Yellowstone National Park. By John Hyde. Cloth, $1.00; paper	.50
The Mexican Guide. By Thos. A. Janvier. Revised yearly	2.50

Any book sent postpaid on receipt of price. Besides the above partial list we keep in stock a large selection of Guide Books, Maps, and works of reference for tourists and travelers. We publish pocket maps of all the American States and Territories, the Canadian Provinces, and Foreign Countries, and can furnish maps and guides to every country and every important city in the world.

Send for complete list to

RAND, McNALLY & CO.,
MAP AND BOOK PUBLISHERS.
148 TO 154 MONROE ST., CHICAGO.

THE RIALTO SERIES

The books of this series are all works of special merit, and are either copyright productions of American authors, or noteworthy writings of foreign authors.

They are bound in neat and modest paper covers, at **50 cts.** each; and most of them also in tasteful cloth bindings, with gold back and side titles, at **$1.00** each, postpaid.

The paper series being entered at the Chicago Post Office is mailable at one cent a pound.

The Dream (Le Rêve). By E. ZOLA. Illustrated. Paper and Cloth.
The Iron Master (Le Maître de Forges). By GEORGES OHNET. Illustrated. Paper and cloth.
The Blackhall Ghosts. By SARAH TYTLER.
The Immortal, or one of the "Forty" (L'Immortel). By A. DAUDET. Illustrated. Paper and cloth.
Marriage and Divorce. By AP RICHARD and others. Paper and cloth.
Daniel Trentworthy; a Tale of the Great Fire. By JOHN McGOVERN. Typogravure Illustrations. Paper and cloth.
The Silence of Dean Maitland. By MAXWELL GREY. Paper and cloth.
Nikanor. By HENRY GREVILLE. Translated by MRS. E. E. CHASE. Typogravure Illustrations. Cloth and Paper.
Dr. Rameau. By GEORGES OHNET. Illustrated. Paper and cloth.
The Slaves of Folly. By WM. HORACE BROWN. Cloth and Paper.
Merze; The Story of an Actress. By MARAH ELLIS RYAN. Typogravure Illustrations. Cloth and paper.
My Uncle Barbassou. By MARIO UCHARD. Illustrated. Paper and cloth.
Up Terrapin River. By OPIE P. READ. Cloth and paper.

LATER LISTS CAN BE HAD ON APPLICATION.

RAND, McNALLY & CO.,
PUBLISHERS,
148 to 154 Monroe St., **CHICAGO**

323 Broadway, NEW YORK.

www.ingramcontent.com/pod-product-compliance
Lightning Source LLC
Chambersburg PA
CBHW032113230426
43672CB00009B/1728